THE MUSEUM EXPERIENCE

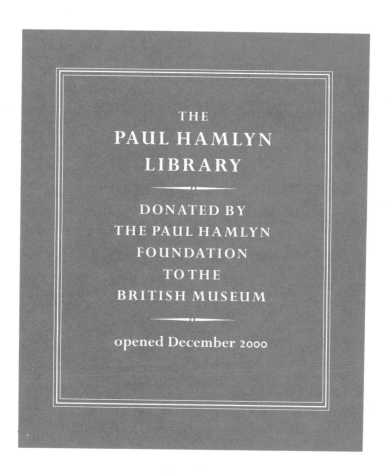

THE
MUSEUM
EXPERIENCE

John H. Falk
Lynn D. Dierking

Foreword by
Willard L. Boyd

WHALESBACK BOOKS
WASHINGTON, D.C.

Edited by Mellen Candage
Book and Cover designed by Anne Meagher-Cook
Printed (alk paper) and bound in the US by
Edwards Brothers, Ann Arbor, Michigan

Library of Congress Cataloguing-in-Publication Data

Falk, John H. (John Howard), 1948–   .
   The museum experience / John H. Falk. Lynn D. Dierking:
foreword by Willard L. Boyd.
      p. cm.
   Includes bibliographical references.
   ISBN 0-929590-06-6: 36.00.—ISBN 0-929590-07-4 (pbk.): 17.95
   1. Museums—Educational aspects. I. Dierking, Lynn D. (Lynn
Diane), 1956–   . Title.
AM7.F35 1992
069'.15—dc20   91-44108
                                                              CIP

WHALESBACK BOOKS IS AN IMPRINT OF HOWELLS HOUSE
BOX 9546 WASHINGTON, DC 20016

To Mac Laetsch and John Koran,
with thanks for their guidance and support.

Contents

Foreword

The Museum Experience is one of the most stimulating and readable books I have ever encountered. It is about lifelong learning, a subject second only to the weather in concern.

Throughout a lifetime as an educator, in a university and in a museum, I have been amazed by the lack of clearly presented analyses to help educators be more effective. This book goes far to fill that void. It moves beyond anecdotes to concepts in a cogent manner to allow us to evaluate and understand learning in museums.

Nowadays, the effectiveness of every type of educational institution is in question. Museums are no exception. *The Museum Experience* provides both the insight and the framework for every museum to review its educational effectiveness.

Unlike schools and universities, museums have difficulty in articulating their educational mission. This is particularly ironic because museums had their origins as centers of learning. Early American colleges and universities were organized around cabinets of natural history and galleries of art. Moreover, freestanding museums have always sought "educational" status under tax and other laws.

Today, most American museums reject the approach of the curator in Louis Auchincloss's *The Golden Calves*, who says, "Ah, educational! The holy word. You'd think we had no more schools or colleges. I thought museums were for the educated."

Conversely, we have to beware the other extreme, which denies the vital research role which many museums have. Like universities, some museums have the inseparable missions of basic research and public education.

The Museum Experience focuses on the public learning role, which requires rigorous analysis and systematic planning. Museums have much to learn in order to serve a wide public effectively. Currently, we serve a narrow audience. Most museum visitors are relatively well educated. This self-selecting audience, coupled with the inwardly driven institutional perspective, has kept museums from serving a diverse public in an environment of changing educational techniques. The challenge of serving a broad public constituency and adopting new exhibit approaches produces the healthy debate and tension reflected in the museum field today. It is said that showmanship is replacing scholarship in museums. The issue is not showmanship versus scholarship; rather, the issue is how to convey scholarship to a diverse public.

The conditions of museum learning are very different from those of the classroom. Museum learning is self-directed rather than directed by a teacher. Exhibits replace the teacher as the central medium of instruction. Objects instead of words are the principal currency of discourse. Visitors need not satisfy any academic prerequisites to be admitted to a museum. Museums award no credit for completing an exhibit. There is no compulsory attendance law, career placement office, or even beloved teacher to induce attendance. The object is not to graduate visitors, but rather to have them stay in the exhibits longer, learn more, and return to the museum frequently throughout their lifetimes.

The Museum Experience systematically examines the conditions for museum learning from the appropriate perspective: the multiplicity of visitors' points of view. Visitors must be motivated and engaged if they are to learn and want to return. Motivation and engagement are the basic elements of effective education in all settings. While the passive large-section lecture is more efficient in communicating quantities of information, the participatory seminar is more effective in stimulating student curiosity and understanding. Similarly, museum visitors learn more and return more when they are actively engaged.

John Falk and Lynn Dierking make it clear that more effective museum learning requires rigorous planning and evaluation. Their visitor examples are humbling, but should not lead to despair because less is specifically remembered from college lectures than from museum visits.

America's museums have contributed much to public learning. They can and must contribute much more. *The Museum Experience* is an invaluable means to that end. This compact volume is a lucid and germane enumeration of the basic issues of visitor learning. It will have resonance for every museum professional—because every museum professional is vitally concerned with the museum's central role as a center of public learning.

Willard L. Boyd
President, Field Museum of
Natural History
Chicago, October 22, 1991

Preface

Museums have expanded in variety and exploded in popularity over the last few decades. As their numbers and popularity have grown, there has been a marked change in the role of the museum in society. Whereas museums have historically been oriented primarily toward collections and research, they now are increasingly viewed by the public as institutions for public learning. All museums now place an emphasis on education that they never did in the past.*

The first museums were private collections, shared with others selectively by the collector. Visits were conducted privately, and the issue of "educating the public" did not arise. Over time, the role of the museum as a public asset became increasingly important, but for many it remained a secondary function.

The changes in the focus and character of museums are complicated ones, far better explained by historians, and certainly not in the purview of this book, but the significance of the transformation is undisputed. Whereas a quarter of a century ago most museums would have listed "education" as a distant third on their list of institutional priorities, behind collections and research, these same museums would now be inclined to state that they are, first and foremost, centers for public learning—or, at the very least, equally concerned about education, research, and collections. Collections and research remain important in the museum world,

---

*In this book, "museums" are defined as historical homes and sites; science and technology and nature centers; aquaria, zoos, and botanical gardens; as well as the traditional art, history, and natural history museums.

and in many older institutions curators and registrars retain significant clout. Still, in the brief space of a generation, institutional priorities have, in many cases, been turned upside down. Associate directors or vice presidents for education and public programming have suddenly appeared in institutions where there was once only a single "education coordinator" consigned to the basement. During this same period, hundreds of new museums without collections were established—solely for the purpose of educating the public. The expectation is that, increasingly, all museum professionals, from directors and educators to exhibition designers and curators, will need to know how to communicate information to the public.

Although museums have been around for a very long time, the public aspect of the museum world is relatively new. According to Edward Able, Executive Director of the American Association of Museums, attendance at U.S. museums doubled from 200 million in 1965 to nearly 400 million in 1984, and topped 500 million a few years later.[1] Attendance figures continue to increase. Museum-going is rapidly becoming the single most popular, out-of-home family activity in America.[2] This boom reflects a phenomenal increase in the total number of museums as well as increased attendance. Hand in hand with increases in numbers and popularity, museums have experienced rapid increases in the level of financial support they receive.

These are only a few of the changes in the museum world. Whereas, historically, museums were supported largely by private money and a modicum of public funds, today, most of the financial support for museums comes from the public sector. Public money comes with significant strings attached, many of which require attainment of public education goals. Moreover, whereas museums used to receive considerable support from personal contributions, private-sector support now comes primarily from corporations. Like public money, corporate money has strings attached: No longer content with recognition derived from naming a building, corporations want to be sure that their contributions, essentially promotional expenditures, are highly visible to the public. Funds are most likely to be given for the development of programs or exhibitions that will ensure that large numbers of people will know who supported the endeavor.

These educational mandates have required the recognition of museums as significant learning environments. Consequently, it has become difficult to attend a museum conference without hearing the word "learning." Museum professionals have sought a better understanding of learning theory and learning styles, but their efforts in many cases have led to confusion, because learning is a much-used, much-abused term, meaning very different things to different people. What is learning, and how can it be said that the museum experience is a learning experience? These are questions we will address in this book.

We have organized the book in the same way that we have attempted to understand the museum experience, that is, from the visitor's perspective. We can view the museum experience as a timeline—a journey from a person's first thought of visiting a museum, through the actual visit, and then beyond, when the museum experience remains only in memory. We have focused not on what visitors *should* do and remember, but on what they actually do and remember.

The first step in understanding the museum visitor's experience is to ask why, of all the possible ways an individual or family could spend leisure time, millions of people freely choose to visit museums. The first section of this book addresses the reasons people come to museums and what they expect to do there.

Once inside a museum, many choices of where to go and what to see present themselves. How do people behave inside museums? What is the interplay among the visitor's social group, the immediate experience (such as exhibit content and design), and factors such as the visitor's previous knowledge, interests, and expectations? The second section of the book addresses the issue of what people do from the time they walk through the front door of a museum until the time they exit, and what influences their behavior.

For most people, a museum visit is just one of many

experiences in a day, week, and lifetime of experiences. Yet everyone who enters a museum and spends any appreciable time there is affected. What do people remember about a museum visit? Drawing from a variety of research studies by a multitude of investigators, the third section of the book attempts to piece together a coherent picture of the effect of the museum experience on a visitor, focusing in particular on whether the museum visit can be considered a learning experience.

In the last section of the book, we provide a guide to the museum experience for the museum professional. In this section we make the transition from the visitor's perspective to the museum's perspective. We have tried to use what we have learned about the museum experience to inform the practice of museum interpretation and exhibition design. We recommend ways to enhance the visitor's museum experience and to help museums accomplish their educational agendas. Finally, we have selected a number of references for annotation. These works were significant publications for us, important in our understanding of the museum experience.

This book is an attempt to present the "big picture" of the common, but still poorly understood, use by the public of places like science centers, art museums, history museums, historical homes, nature centers, aquaria, botanical gardens, and zoos. The book is not an exhaustive survey of research about museums; instead, it presents a framework, based on the existing body of research, within which to view the museum experience. To this end we have devised what we call the Interactive Experience Model.

We have spent the better part of the last twenty years working in science centers, museums, zoos, botanical gardens, and nature centers. Like most education-oriented museum professionals, we have devoted much of our energy to trying to improve the visitor's museum experience. The ideas discussed in this book and the issues raised are ones that we have thought long and hard about over many years. The opinions expressed are our own. We hope they will be provocative and will encourage discussion and debate in the field.

This book represents many years of effort, several spent in the writing and many more in the trenches, watching visitors, talking to visitors, and, equally if not more importantly, talking with other researchers and educators. To these people we are grateful. We would particularly like to thank our long-time colleague and friend John Balling, who was a co-investigator on many of our early studies and provided many years' worth of ideas and suggestions for the book. He should be recognized as a true pioneer in the research on understanding visitor behavior.

In addition, we are grateful to those many individuals who, over the years, have shared their insights and thoughts with us. In no particular order, we wish to thank Mac Laetsch, Judy Diamond, Mick Alt, John J. Koran, Jr., Chandler Screven, Mike Templeton, Stephen Bitgood, S. M. Nair, Arthur Lucas, Roger Miles, George Hein, Sam Taylor, Hope Jensen Leichter, Randi Korn, and Paulette McManus.

We owe special gratitude to those who reviewed drafts of the book and provided suggestions—some of the best and brightest thinkers in the field today. For taking the time to read various versions of the manuscript and making valuable comments, we wish to thank D. D. Hilke, Judy White, Harris Shettel, Gail Leeds, Ken Yellis, Gloria Gerace, Bonnie Van Dorn, Janet Kamien, Nancy McCoy, Susan McCormick, Linda Deck, Elaine Neuman Gurian, and Mary Alexander.

Willard ("Sandy") Boyd provided valuable comments and, even more importantly, a generous foreword for which we are extremely grateful.

Introduction:
The Interactive
Experience Model

This book examines the way the public uses museums. It seeks to understand museums from a visitor's perspective. Millions of people, young and old, alone and in groups, have some kind of museum experience every year. This is a book about that experience, the total experience, from the moment the thought occurs to someone to go to a museum, through the remembrance of the museum visit, days, weeks, and years later. Why do people go to museums? What do they do once they are in the museum? What do they remember afterwards?

Throughout this book we use the term "museum" to refer to a wide range of informal educational institutions, including art, history, and natural history museums; zoos; arboretums; botanical gardens; science centers; historic homes; and a variety of other exhibits and collections. Many common strands run through the museum experience, regardless of the type of institution, and different types of visitors manifest distinct patterns of behavior. These patterns depend on a number of variables, including the frequency of attendance, the expectations with which visitors arrive, and the knowledge and experience they bring to bear upon their visit. In an attempt to present a coherent picture of the visitor's total museum experience, we have created a framework for making sense of both the common strands and the unique complexities of the museum experience, the similarities and differences among museums and among visitors. We call this framework the Interactive

Experience Model. We have found this model to be a useful framework within which to organize and interpret the wealth of research and information that make up the museum visitor literature, as well as relevant research from psychology, anthropology, and sociology. Throughout this book, we use the Interactive Experience Model as a lens through which we view and try to make sense of museum visits and experiences.

Given the multiplicity of visitor and museum types, trying to understand why visitors go to museums, what they do there, and what they will remember is a significant challenge. We have approached this effort from a visitor's perspective and have conceptualized the museum visit as involving an interaction among three contexts:

1) The personal context;
2) The social context; and
3) The physical context.

All museum visits involve these three contexts; they are the windows through which we can view the visitor's perspective.

The Personal Context

Each museum visitor's personal context is unique; it incorporates a variety of experiences and knowledge, including varying degrees of experience in and knowledge of the content and design of the museum. The personal context also includes the visitor's interests, motivations, and concerns. Such characteristics help to mold what an individual enjoys and appreciates, how he wishes to spend his time, and what experiences he seeks for self-fulfillment. These characteristics also mean that each person arrives at the museum with a personal agenda—a set of expectations and anticipated outcomes for the visit. Differences in personal context, for example, should help predict many of the differences in visitor behavior and learning that exist, for example, between first-time and frequent visitors, or between novices and experts in a given subject matter.

The Social Context

Visits to museums occur within a social context. Most people visit museums in a group, and those who visit alone invariably come into contact with other visitors and museum staff. Every visitor's perspective is strongly influenced by social context. The museum experience differs depending on whether one walks through a museum with an eighteen-year-old or with an eighty-year-old in tow; whether one is a parent with two small children; or whether or not one's companion is knowledgeable about the exhibits. Whether or not the museum is crowded also strongly influences the museum experience; so do interactions with museum staff and volunteers. Understanding the social context of the visit allows us to make sense of variations in behavior between, for example, adults in family groups and adults in adult groups, or children on school field trips and children visiting with their families.

The Physical Context

The museum is a physical setting that visitors, usually freely, *choose* to enter. The physical context includes the architecture and "feel" of the building, as well as the objects and artifacts contained within. How visitors behave, what they observe, and what they remember are strongly influenced by the physical context. For example, the smell of the elephant house at a zoo may influence how long certain visitors will spend watching elephants. Carpeting the floor of a museum and adding benches can lessen the fatigue that visitors experience. Many of the distinctions between, for example, an art museum and a science museum, or a historic home and an aquarium, derive from elements of the physical context—the architecture, the objects on display, the ambience—elements that exert significant influence on the visitor.

The Model

Each of the contexts is continuously constructed by the visitor, and the interaction of these create the visitor's experience. This constructed reality is unique to the individual; no two people ever see the world in quite the same way. Julian Jaynes provided perhaps the best analogy when, describing consciousness, he suggested that what we are aware of is like a flashlight in a dark room.[1] We can only see what is illuminated at any given instant; nothing else exists. Three people standing in a dark room, each with his own light focused on the same object, will illuminate the object differently because of the differing nature of their beams (personal context), the angle from which they cast their light (physical context), and the variable benefits of shared light (social context). Similarly, three people standing in front of an exhibit will each have a different experience.

Museum staff design exhibitions, develop label copy, and carefully arrange objects in hope that visitors will attend to them, but that does not always happen. When it does, the visitor's context includes those exhibitions, labels, and objects. When the visitor does not attend to an exhibition, label, or object, they do not become part of the visitor's immediate context—his constructed experience. Whatever the visitor does attend to is filtered through the personal context, mediated by the social context, and embedded within the physical context. Viewing the process in terms of the interaction of visitor-constructed contexts helps us recognize that the choices visitors make—such as watching a film or listening to a lecture-demonstration, visiting when the museum is crowded or empty, seeing the dinosaurs or the mummies first, walking around the museum a little longer or stopping for lunch—make the difference between a *potential* museum experience and the *actual* one.

The Interactive-Experience Model can be visualized as a three-dimensional set of three interacting spheres, each representing one of the three contexts (see Figure 1). The museum experience occurs within the physical context, a collection of structures and things we call the museum. Within the museum is the visitor, who perceives the world through his own personal context. Sharing this experience are various other people, each with their own personal context, which together create a social context. At any given

THE
INTERACTIVE
EXPERIENCE
MODEL

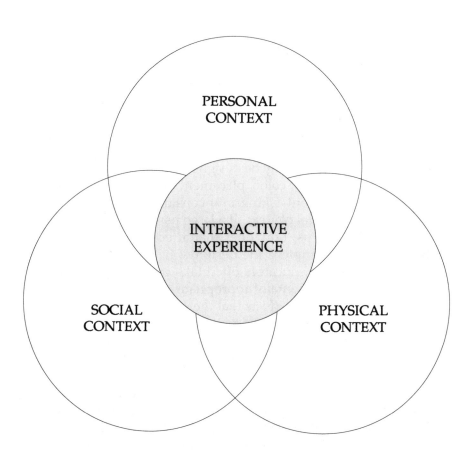

moment, the visitor focuses on a particular object, individual, or thought, or, more likely, several of these simultaneously. The relative sizes of the spheres, as depicted in Figure 1, do not necessarily represent the relative importance of the three contexts. At any given moment, any one of the three contexts could assume major importance in influencing the visitor. The visitor's experience can be thought of as a continually shifting interaction among personal, social, and physical contexts. The visitor's experience can be represented by a series of snapshots, each freezing in time a moment of interaction of the three contextual components. The Interactive Experience Model predicts that a visitor's experience can best be understood by looking, over time, at the series of critical intersections of the three contexts.

The museum experience has not been viewed in this way in the past. Most museum professionals, whether educators, designers, or curators, have viewed the museum experience as a subset of this model rather than as the whole. For example, exhibits may be designed with careful attention to aspects of lighting, color, placement of objects, and readability of text without taking into consideration the important role of the social context. If a large percentage of visitors are in family groups, how does that affect readability of labels? Another example is the design of field trips for school children. Museum educators often take great pains to make the lesson developmentally appropriate and relevant to exhibitions, but ignore the effects that the novelty of the museum setting might have on children. These oversights are the result of an incomplete model of the museum experience, a focus on the interaction of just two contexts, or an incomplete appreciation of what constitutes a context.

It is possible to take a limited contextual perspective and still arrive at interesting conclusions about visitor behavior in museums. Many researchers have in fact done this. It may even be sometimes justifiable or necessary to take a narrow perspective in order to ferret out some particularly important interaction. But limiting one's view of the contexts involved does result in distortions, and the results from research so conducted need to be analyzed carefully to account for these.

The Interactive Experience Model suggests that all three contexts should contribute significantly to the museum experience, though not necessarily in equal proportion in all cases. The model also predicts that, although the three contexts can be viewed separately, they function, in fact, as an integrated whole. This book uses the Interactive Experience Model to provide a perspective for understanding the visitor's total experience—a socially, physically, intellectually, and emotionally rich experience.

SECTION I
Before the Visit

1.
The Museum as a Leisure-Time Experience

Millions of people each year enter a museum. For most people, visiting a museum, zoo, nature center, or science center is an enjoyable way to spend leisure time, one involving family or friends on weekends, vacations, or free time during the week. Some come in small groups or individually; some arrive as part of an organized group, participating in a pre-planned visit. Millions of children visit museums each year on school field trips, for example, and more and more elderly adults now visit museums as part of scheduled trips.

Placing themselves within a "physical context" is not how most people think of a museum visit, but that is what they have done. Visitors consciously choose a place to go, a place where they can expect certain kinds of experiences whether they will be the exertion of athletics at a gym or a sports field, the thrills of a roller coaster at an amusement park, the drama of a movie or play at a theater, or the edification of exhibits at a museum. The setting selected depends a great deal on the social and personal needs to be fulfilled. In the Interactive Experience Model, it is the physical context that provides many of the constants of experience. Museum settings are designed to provide visitors with predictable and specific experiences. Visitors go to an aquarium expecting to see live fish in tanks and to read information about them. Visitors go to an art museum expecting to see paintings hung on walls, often very specific paintings. Though obvious, this perspective is important. Embedded in the relationship between the physical context and the personal context is an unspoken contract of expectations. What expectations associated with museums result in a decision to visit or not to visit? This question forms the essence of the next chapter, but first, some basic questions must be addressed: Who are museum visitors, and why do they choose to spend their free time in museums?

We can determine who visits museums relatively easily from direct observation of the visiting population. Although years of demographic studies have provided profiles of museum visitors, museum-visiting patterns appear to be changing dramatically, and the studies conducted in the 1970s may not reflect accurately the visiting population of twenty years later. The generalizations we make here must be recognized as our current best estimates only, subject to change.

The answer to the question why people visit museums is much more difficult and requires careful analysis; direct observation of visitors will not suffice. The fact that people are visiting museums in ever-greater numbers reflects the changes in the leisure-time marketplace and in our concepts of what constitutes leisure time. Even within this shifting environment, however, some generalizations seem likely to persist over time.

Why People Go To Museums

Many school and other trips to museums take place during the week, but the overwhelming majority of museum visitors come during weekends and vacation periods. Most visitors have made the choice to spend their leisure time visiting a museum. Why does one person choose to visit a museum and another not? The actual amount of discretionary time for most Americans is limited, but the options for the use of that time seem almost unlimited.[1]

In spite of numerous out-of-home attractions, most Americans spend most of their leisure time at home.[2] Favorite activities include gardening, hobbies, exercise, card games, board games, listening to music, reading, talking with friends, and watching television.[3] By the age of eighteen, the average child is estimated to have watched more than 16,000 hours of television—more time than he has spent in school.[4]

The decision to visit a museum involves matching personal and social interests and desires with the anticipated physical context and the associated activities of a museum. Two important considerations in leisure-time decision-making are the investment of time and money, and the importance attached to the activity,[5] in short, the costs and the benefits of any given choice.

Most museums charge an admission fee. Although not a limitation for most Americans, admission fees seem to affect visitor frequency among low income groups.[6] Price is only one of several cost considerations. Time is a major museum "cost." It takes time to get to a museum, and time to walk around it. When time is limited, potential museum visitors must weigh their other commitments against the time required to visit a museum.[7]

Another consideration is convenience. How easy is it to get to the museum? Does it require driving through unfamiliar or unsafe areas of the city? Will traffic be an aggravation? Is parking available? If so, how costly and convenient is it? Will the museum visit coincide with mealtime? If so, is food available? What will it cost, and will it be good? What will the weather be like?

What will be the benefits of visiting the museum? Is the environment pleasant? If it is a nice day, perhaps would it be better to do something outside? Is the museum a place where one will be comfortable, physically and psychologically? If not, is the discomfort going to be worth it? Will one meet new people there? Is it a good place to go with friends or family? Is it someplace where one will learn something? Will one be challenged? Will it be relaxing? Is it safe? Do the facilities accommodate young children? Can one do other things there, such as buy gifts or have good food? Is this such a rare opportunity that one absolutely should not miss the chance to see or do it? Are there things to "do," or is it someplace where one can enjoy being a spectator? Will the experience be intellectually or aesthetically enriching? Will the experience improve social or professional standing? Will it be fun?

Most visitors are unlikely to value all of these potential benefits equally. Museum investigators have tried seriously to define and categorize the *reasons* people visit museums only within the last fifteen years.[8] Typically, visitor responses to the question "Why did you come here today?" can be grouped in three broad categories: (1) social-recreational reasons; (2) educational reasons; and (3) reverential reasons.[9]

Recreational and social considerations consistently rank high among reasons for visiting museums. Studies conducted at the Dallas Museum of Natural History, four Virginia science centers, the San Francisco Zoo, and the Natural History Museum in London, all concluded that visitors were visiting primarily for reasons pertaining to amusement, recreation, fun, and social concerns.[10] Among the top five reasons visitors gave for visiting the Henry Ford Museum and Greenfield Village outside Detroit, Michigan, were family fun and togetherness, a safe environment, and a good place to bring guests, with the first reason the most highly rated.[11] Sherman Rosenfeld distinguished between two competing reasons for a visit to the San Francisco Zoo: content (the animals) and context (the zoo setting.) In his surveys, context dominated; 71 percent of the responses were related to context, whereas only 29 percent were related to content. A follow-up study at a different zoo produced similar results. None of the visitors interviewed cited "learning" as a motivation for going to the zoo.[12]

Harris Shettel (personal communication, 1990) has cautioned against over-interpreting the results of studies such as Rosenfeld's, suggesting that the content (animals) may be too obvious to mention as a reason for visiting a zoo. Because the content of a zoo is animals, learning about animals is implicit and unnecessary to state. Barbara Birney makes the additional point that semantics may be a problem in interpreting studies such as the ones cited above. The public tends to restrict the definition of learning to that which occurs in school. Birney found evidence that visitors *do* come to learn, if we broaden the definition of learning to include the results of curiosity and the urge to explore. There is a constant problem of semantics in studies like this, particularly in the use of the terms "learning" and "education." If we use the broader definition suggested by Birney, learning becomes one of the major motivations for museum visits.[13]

In a survey of approximately 3,000 Americans, Steven Kellert found that "educational benefit to children" was, at 38 percent, the reason most often cited for attendance at zoos and other institutions with animal exhibits.[14] Minda Borun discovered that one or both parents in a significant percentage of families visiting the Franklin Institute in Philadelphia expressed a strong interest in science;[15] Falk found similar results at the California Museum of Science and Industry in Los Angeles and the Maryland Science Center in Baltimore.[16] The desire of parents to extend their interests to their children suggests learning is a major motive for visits to science centers. In the Henry Ford Museum and Greenfield Village survey cited above, learning, specifically the educational benefit for children and enjoyment of history, figured prominently in the other two of the top five reasons for visiting.[17]

Another important source of attraction for visitors is a unique or unusual museum display. In some cases, the museums themselves are considered unique or national treasures, such as the Smithsonian Institution in Washington, D.C.; in other cases, they present unique or special objects or exhibits. Many people feel obligated to depart from normal leisure patterns to see displays such as the King Tut or first moon rock exhibits, or national monuments.

Anthropologist Nelson Graburn has alluded to the public's need for reverential experience, "a personal experience with something higher, more sacred, and out of the ordinary than home and work are able to supply."[18] The museum can offer something akin to a religious experience, and can be a place of "peace and fantasy" where the visitor can escape the mundane, work-a-day world. There are few data to support or refute this idea, but Ken Yellis was able to find evidence that, among certain frequent visitors to art museums, at least, the "reverential" motivation is considerable.[19] In a series of focus group interviews conducted at eleven major art museums, "reverence" emerged as an important ingredient for at least some of the visitors.[20]

Although museums clearly offer social-recreational, educational, and reverential benefits, the question remains why some choose a museum while others choose another venue for these benefits. To address this question, we must look at museum visits in the broader context of leisure options.

In their study of New England residents' leisure activities, William Gudykunst and colleagues found that people could be categorized according to the decisions they made about how to spend their leisure time.[21] They described three categories that embraced people's leisure-time orientation: (1) "cultural or intellectual"; (2) "organization or club"; and (3) "participation."

Gudykunst noted that those people who tended to choose leisure-time activities from the "cultural or intellectual" category—concert-going, theater, movies, reading for pleasure, and traveling and touring—were the same people who tended to be museum-goers. Other studies have confirmed a high correlation between people who visit museums and those who attend concerts and plays.[22] In contrast, people whose leisure-time activities tend toward organizations and clubs are not regular museum-goers; nor are those in the third category, "participation," which includes people who enjoy participation in sports, games, and dancing. Overall, Gudykunst found relatively little overlap among individuals in these three groups.[23]

Marilyn Hood, in a more detailed analysis of leisure-time decision-making,[24] describes six major criteria by which individuals judge leisure activities:

1) Being with people, or social interaction;
2) Doing something worthwhile;
3) Feeling comfortable and at ease in one's surroundings;

4) Having a challenge of new experiences;

5) Having an opportunity to learn; and

6) Participating actively.

In selecting a leisure-time activity, people normally look for something that involves a combination of these criteria, but not all six. At the Toledo Art Museum, Hood studied the criteria that were instrumental in the leisure-time decisions of three groups: (1) frequent museum-goers (three or more visits per year); (2) those who did not visit museums; and (3) occasional visitors (once or twice per year). These three "populations" (as they are called by researchers) made decisions about their leisure-time activities on the basis of very different criteria.

The frequent visitors, some of whom visited the Toledo Art Museum as often as forty times per year, highly valued all six of the criteria and, significantly, perceived that museums were places that could satisfy all six. Hence, it was not surprising that they chose to visit museums often. Of the six attributes, the three most important to this group were opportunities to learn, challenge of new experiences, and doing something worthwhile.

Hood determined that people with this leisure profile represented only 14 percent of the total adult population of Toledo, but they accounted for nearly half of all the Toledo Art Museum's visits. For this population, museums were satisfying places to visit because the three leisure criteria they valued most highly were embodied in museums. The benefits of museum-going for this group consistently outweighed costs such as time, money, travel, or fatigue. They typically visited museums wherever they were and reported that, when they traveled, visiting museums in a new city was a high priority. People in this group were as likely to visit the museum alone as with another person. Hood's population of frequent visitors seems similar to Gudykunst's category (1), "cultural or intellectual" group.

People who did not visit museums made up 46 percent of the Toledo population, and the three leisure-time criteria *most* important to this group were the three of *least* importance to the frequent visitors—being with people,

participating actively, and feeling at ease in their surroundings. The three criteria ranked highest by the frequent visitors
(learning, challenges, worthwhileness) were actually ranked
as unimportant by people who did not visit museums.

The population that did not visit museums believed that
the three criteria they valued most highly were, for the most
part, not present in museums. They perceived museums as
environments that restricted activity and were socially and
physically uncomfortable. Museums were described by this
group as formal, formidable places that were physically or
socially inaccessible to them. This group preferred to spend
out-of-home leisure time participating in or watching sports,
picnicking, or going to shopping malls. As described by
Hood, this group seems to be similar to the group in
Gudykunst's third category, which tends to choose "participation" activities in leisure time.

The third group Hood studied—occasional visitors—
was an interesting group. This group accounted for roughly
40 percent of Toledo's population, and their one or two visits
per year to the art museum accounted for half the museum's
visits.

Occasional visitors shared more characteristics with
people who did not visit museums than they did with frequent museum-goers. In fact, they valued most highly the
same three leisure-time criteria as did people who didn't go
to museums—being with people, participating actively, and
feeling at ease in their surroundings. They appeared to have
begun participatory activities early in life, and continued to
prefer such activities in their adult years. Occasional visitors
enjoyed activities such as camping, hiking, swimming, ski-
ing, boating, skating, playing musical instruments, engaging
in arts and crafts, going to amusement parks or movies,
sightseeing, and attending sporting events. Places of high
appeal to this group were parks, zoos, picnic areas, outdoor
art and music festivals—all good places for families. Like the
group that did not go to museums, this group greatly enjoyed family-centered activities.

Whereas people who were not museum-goers believed
that museums did not offer the three criteria they valued

most highly, occasional visitors felt that museums did have some of these attributes. With other competing leisure-time activities, however, they opted to visit museums only occasionally. Occasional museum-goers were, therefore, most likely to visit museums during special exhibitions, museum-sponsored family events, or at special times, such as when they were entertaining an out-of-town visitor. Hood suggests that this group in particular seemed to equate "leisure" with "relaxation," which is "more akin to interacting socially with a family or friendship group than it is to the intense involvement in a special interest that is evidenced by a museum enthusiast."[25] There is probably also some overlap between this group and Gudykunst's second and third groups, as some individuals in those groups might attend museums, but not as many as in his "intellectual or cultural" group.

Hood comments that museum professionals' values tend to be more in line with those of frequent visitors; hence, museums generally offer or emphasize the very qualities that are least appealing to occasional and non-visiting populations. For example, "selling" the museum as an extension of school (in fact, emphasizing learning at all) might entice frequent participants, but could deter occasional visitors and be a reason for non-participants to avoid museums. Museums that promote themselves as good places for families to explore, discover, and enjoy each other in a relaxed setting would be more likely to draw visitors from among the groups that do not visit, or visit only occasionally.

Determining visitor motivation for visiting a museum is even more complex than determining overall leisure-time motivation. Visitors to the Henry Ford Museum and Green-field Village were surveyed in a series of marketing studies to learn more about the factors that influenced their visits to the museum.[26] One question posed to visitors was: "How would you describe your visit to a friend?" Frequent visitors to the Henry Ford Museum were most likely to answer that it was "fun" and a "great museum to visit"; less frequent visitors tended to answer that it was "educational." At first glance, the responses seem to fly in the face of Hood's conclusions, which would predict exactly the opposite response.

It is possible, however, that for frequent visitors, "fun" *is* "educational," and that for less frequent visitors, who do not regard educational activities as fun, the answer explained their infrequent visitor status. Despite considerable progress in recent years in our understanding of leisure-time behavior, particularly as regards museums, clearly much still remains to be learned.

Who Visits Museums

According to the U.S. Bureau of the Census, 347.8 million people visited museums in 1985.[27] Five years later, the American Association of Museums (AAM) estimated the number at around 500 million per year.[28] Myriad demographic studies of museum visitors have been conducted over the years in an attempt to specify the age and social profile of visitors.[29] The results of these studies are relatively consistent: Most people who visit museums go in a family group, with parents between the ages of thirty and fifty and children between the ages of eight and twelve. Most museum visitors are white, middle-class, well educated, and reasonably affluent. Seventy percent of the visitors to the British Natural History Museum who were not in school groups came in other social groups, of which 60 percent were family groups.[30] A similar pattern has been observed at museums in the United States.[31] Families and children are most frequently found at children's museums, followed by zoo and science and technology centers. Fewer families and children visit natural history and history museums. At art museums, families and children are rare. Family groups at science centers, for example, may constitute as much as 80 percent of all visitors, while at art museums it is not uncommon for families to represent less than 10 percent of all visitors.[32]

Yet most museum visitors, young or old, come as part of a social group. When not accompanied by children, adults usually come with other adults. According to numerous surveys of visitors conducted in museums during the 1970s and 1980s,[33] adults make up from 30 to as much as 90 percent of visitors, depending upon the type of institution. Most adult visitors are under sixty years of age; adults over sixty rarely constitute more than 10 percent of the visiting public. Most visitors are between the ages of thirty-five and fifty. More males than females tend to visit science museums; more females than males visit art museums.

Although some people maintain a steady pace of museum-going throughout their lives, others visit primarily when their leisure time and interests make museum visits most appropriate. J. R. Kelly has stated that patterns of leisure activities, such as museum-going, are generally learned through a process of socialization.[34] According to Kelly, the family is the most significant influence in learning leisure activities.

People learn that different activities reinforce their lifestyles and desires at different times of their lives. For example, many people associate museum visits with their childhoods because their parents took them to museums when they were children. As they became adolescents and young adults, they focused more on athletic or club events. But when they became parents, they returned to museums for the benefit of their children. Kelly states that parents resume about half of the activities they themselves participated in when they were young.

Visitor surveys consistently suggest that, by and large, museum visitors are of higher than average socioeconomic level.[35] These findings apply equally to visitors of art museums, science museums, arboreta, and zoos; they apply as well cross-culturally, to visitors in the U.S.A., Canada, Sweden, and Great Britain. For example, research done in Sweden showed that museum visitors have a "considerably higher socioeconomic status than the population in general."[36] Individuals whose education did not extend beyond primary school, and those belonging to the working class or farming population, were most under-represented in a survey of Swedish museum-goers. Education, however, appeared to be a far greater determinant of museum-going than did income, employment, or hobbies.

A recent study at the Royal Ontario Museum found

that its visiting public was well educated and well informed in the area of European art.[37] Many of the visitors had experience in fine arts, textiles, or crafts and had taken courses in art history, medieval history, the Renaissance, or the Industrial Revolution. Although the correlation between high socioeconomic status and high museum attendance almost certainly exists, careful scrutiny of the demographic data, particularly of Hood's, suggests there may be a strong correlation between two "independent" variables—museum popularity and socioeconomic factors. Different kinds of museums attract different types of visitors. Hence, reports that the socioeconomic status of visitors to a particular institution is "average" may be misleading.

Every museum draws a variety of visitors. Consequently, "averages" are a poor way to express the demographics of museum visitors. People in high socioeconomic brackets tend to visit all kinds of museums frequently. People in moderate socioeconomic brackets visit only certain kinds of museums, and these infrequently. People in low socioeconomic brackets tend to visit only the most popular kinds of museums, e.g., zoos or national parks, and these only rarely if at all. Art museums are generally assumed to draw visitors of higher status than do zoos. Although the evidence supports this hypothesis, the data would be better interpreted to suggest who *does not* visit art museums, rather than who *does* visit zoos. The fact is that the number of people in high socioeconomic brackets visiting zoos and art museums may be comparable (some may even be the same people), because a relatively constant number of people in high socioeconomic brackets attend *all* museum settings.

The difference in "average" socioeconomic status between visitors to art museums and visitors to zoos is more highly correlated with the popularity of the museum than with the status of the visitor; it is more a function of how many visitors from the moderate and low socioeconomic segments of the population are attracted, than of how many upper-income people visit. These seemingly subtle distinctions have profound importance for museums in their fundraising efforts and in efforts to enhance museum attendance.

Few hard data exist on the ethnic makeup of museum audiences. Few museum professionals would dispute the fact that racial minorities are under-represented among museum-goers. The few studies that have been done generally substantiate this assumption.[38] Museum visitors in the U.S.A. are now, and historically have been, primarily white. Evidence, also preliminary, suggests that this trend is changing,[39] but for many in the museum community, the change is much too slow and far too haphazard.[40]

Generalizations about the profile of museum visitors—whether generalizations of age, sex, education, or any other characteristic—can be misleading. There is good evidence to suggest that museums attract different types of visitors at different times of year.[41] As museums have invested more time in understanding their publics, they have discovered certain patterns in their visits. For example, summer months often attract more occasional and out-of-town visitors; winter months attract more frequent and local residents.[42] Hood rightly pointed out that visitors had different expectations, according to the season, of arboretum content; moreover, their degree of satisfaction with the arboretum differed accordingly. Therefore, she concluded that " . . . a one-time or one-season assessment of an [arboretum's] audience is insufficient to gauge the diversity of visitor responses."[43] The same could be said of most other institutions.

Ultimately, museum-going behavior appears to depend upon who a person is, demographically speaking, and what he is looking for in the way of leisure-time activity. In fact, if we can define the "who," we should be able to predict whether or not he or she will go to a museum at all and, if so, how frequently and for what reasons. Key factors appear to be age, education, income, race, museum experience, specific interest in topics covered by the museum, social responsibilities such as family or a visiting relative, and general leisure-time preferences. All of these factors can be examined within the framework of the Interactive Experience Model.

The key factors are encompassed in the personal context part of the model—in fact, these factors define the personal context. Given a personal context that predisposes one to use leisure time for intellectually challenging experiences, and given an appropriate social motivation (e.g., Aunt Bertha is spending the day), one is likely to elect to visit a museum because it can satisfy both leisure preferences and social concerns. Further, it promises to accommodate these needs within a safe, stimulating, and enjoyable environment. Another person with a comparable social need but different personal context may opt to take Aunt Bertha to the shopping mall. The shopping mall is also a safe, stimulating, enjoyable environment, but it satisfies different leisure preferences.

Thus, personal context is an excellent predictor of museum attendance. The opposite is equally true. Knowing, for example, that a person is a regular art museum visitor offers excellent insight into a person's education, background, and interests. An individual's personal context not only informs us about his or her predilection to visit museums; it also, in large measure, determines the interests and expectations he or she will bring to the museum. We will look closely at this aspect of personal context in the next chapter.

2.
The Personal Context: Visitor Agendas

As visitors arrive at the museum, they appear happy and expectant, eager to begin their exploration. Most visitors arrive with expectations about what will actually occur. What do they hope to find here? What are their expectations for the experience, and how do these influence the visit itself?

At the heart of every visitor's preconceptions and expectations is her personal context—her personal reservoir of knowledge, attitudes, and experience, influenced by expectations concerning the physical characteristics of the museum, what she will find there, what she can do there, and who is accompanying her on this visit. All these factors merge to create an agenda for the visit. Evidence suggests that this agenda is important in determining the nature of a visitor's museum experience.

Some visitors are very knowledgeable about specific aspects of the museum collection; others are relatively uninformed. Some visitors, even if lacking in subject matter knowledge, are curious about the objects and ideas represented by the museum; some are not. Some visitors are experienced museum-goers; some are not. Some visitors learn best when they touch things; some visitors learn best by reading. Some visitors have phobias—fears of snakes, heights, enclosed spaces, or crowds—that they bring with them on the visit. Some visitors will go to a museum only with other people; some visitors strongly prefer to visit museums alone. All these factors, and more, make up the visitor's personal context and strongly influence the visitor's museum agenda.

When asked about their expectations, family museum visitors at several institutions responded that they expected to find things to do that everyone in the family would enjoy; that they would find an attractive, friendly, safe environment; that they would see something that they had not seen before; and that they would have an opportunity to do more than just look at things, but rather would get to be personally involved with the exhibitions.[1] How were these expectations generated? How much can they be influenced?

Previous Experience

For some visitors, expectations are molded by earlier visits to the institution, as well as visits to other, comparable institutions. Based on first-hand experience, frequent visitors continually define and refine their expectations of what to see and what to do. Every visit to a museum clarifies the scope and potential sequence of the next visit. Repeat visitors to the same museum not only know what to expect and how to locate it, but also which parts and activities of the museum they enjoy and which they do not. Over time, they learn which sections of the institution are crowded and which sections are not, when the museum is busy and when it is quiet. They often become museum members and get on mailing lists. They learn when special events are happening or new exhibitions are opening. All of these things contribute to highly specific expectations.

Nearly everyone has been to the movies often enough to know what to expect in that setting. The only significant unknown is the film to be seen, and that can be determined by reading the movie section of the paper, looking at the marquee outside the theater, or calling the theater. Even when we attend a film in a theater we have never visited before, our expectations focus more on the film than the theater. This is because we have been to so many movies that we have come to expect certain amenities in a movie theater—rest rooms; concessions selling candy, soda, and popcorn; a darkened room with reasonably comfortable seats, etc. We take these things for granted. Similarly, repeat visitors to museums not only know what to expect, but they take many things for granted.

Repeat visitors are different from others not because they have well-formed expectations, but because their expectations are formed by direct and repeated museum experience. When these expectations are not met, such visitors can become highly critical. For example, some long-time visitors to the Natural History Museum in London were outraged when the museum attempted to do away with many exhibitions and displays that had been unchanged for a half-century or more.[2] More recently, visitors raised similar criticisms of changes being made at the Field Museum of Natural History in Chicago and at the American Museum of Natural History in New York City.[3] Most people were critical not because these exhibits were unique and popular; rather, they were upset because the exhibits had always been there, and had become indelibly associated with the institution in their minds. The removal of these exhibits was a breach of the contract of expectations between the regular visitor and the museum. In contrast, first-time visitors to the British Natural History Museum seemed unconcerned at the changes. In fact, when the old and new exhibits were compared, most first-time visitors seemed to prefer the newer exhibitions.[4]

Do first-time or occasional visitors, then, have no expectations? On the contrary, the vast majority of them arrive with definite expectations about what they will do and experience. Sometimes, their expectations are specific. For example, Donald Adams reports that first-time visitors to the Henry Ford Museum and Greenfield Village often arrive expecting, mistakenly, to see all staff in period costumes.[5] Where do these expectations come from? Unlike frequent visitors, first-time visitors' expectations are not based on direct experience. The occasional visitor can draw upon some earlier experience, even if it is only a school field trip or family visit a long time in the past. Although all museum experiences may shape future experiences,[6] current research suggests that occasional visitors are much more like first-time visitors in their expectations of a museum visit, as well as in other ways.[7]

Sources of Information

Most occasional visitors lack recent, direct experience; so where do their expectations come from? They may come from radio or television announcements, public service spots, newspaper articles, or advertising. Most museums regularly put out promotional materials and other forms of publicity in the form of direct mail, posters, hand-outs at libraries or schools, and press releases to the media. But word-of-mouth from friends or relatives who have previously visited the museum appears to be a major, if not *the primary*, vehicle for attracting visitors and forming their expectations. According to Ross Loomis, "a conversational suggestion to visit a museum may well constitute the museum's single most effective source of publicity and public relations."[8]

Adams demonstrated that word-of-mouth appears to be the primary way in which visitors learn about and decide to visit museums.[9] He found that, at the Henry Ford Museum and Greenfield Village, between 1980 and 1988, two-thirds to three-quarters of all visitors indicated that word-of-mouth influenced their decision to visit. Among those visitors who stated they were influenced by word-of-mouth, most were first-time visitors, fewer were occasional visitors, and only a negligible number were frequent visitors.

Colonial Williamsburg, Virginia, estimated that more than 80 percent of first-time visitors and nearly half of repeat visitors originally heard about the institution through word-of-mouth and that it was the single most influential factor in deciding to visit Colonial Williamsburg for three out of four first-time visitors, while subsequent word-of-mouth information was the most important influence for one out of three repeat visitors.[10] Word-of-mouth was also found to be a significant factor in visitors' decisions to visit Franklin Institute, Brandywine River Museum, Conner Prairie Museum, Anniston Museum of Natural History, Biltmore Estate, The Museums of Stony Brook, and Mackinack State Historical Park. For these same institutions, advertising and publicity programs accounted for less than 20 percent of visits.[11]

Word-of-mouth is an important mechanism by which individuals form opinions about their world. A Roper Poll in April 1988 determined that people turn primarily to friends when seeking information that they want to act upon.[12] This is just the kind of information one needs to decide what to do for a leisure-time activity. In a study on consumer habits, word-of-mouth was found to be seven times more effective than newspapers and magazines, four times more effective than personal selling, and twice as effective as radio advertising.[13] In general, word-of-mouth is perceived as a highly credible source of information because it is free from the bias of the people who make, sell, or deliver a product or service.[14] Word-of-mouth reaches people unexpectedly, often in social situations, where people may be especially receptive to recommendations. The social, unsolicited nature of much of word-of-mouth information provides credibility, social validity, and authenticity because it comes from individuals with, presumably, first-hand experience and without a vested interest in what they are recommending. Friends and relatives advise people to visit museums because they believe that the experience will be positive.

The influence of word-of-mouth appears to depend on the source of information; at Henry Ford Museum and Greenfield Village, Adams determined that the most influential sources of word-of-mouth endorsements about the museum were social acquaintances and relatives other than spouses or children. Adams also found that word-of-mouth influenced most heavily first-time visitors, visitors of lower education and income, and visitors from out of town. Those visitors most likely to hear about the Henry Ford Museum through word-of-mouth were also most likely to tell others about the museum after their visit.[15] What were these visitors told to expect at the museum, and did these expectations influence their visit?

Influencing Agendas

How much do a visitor's expectations and previous museum experience affect the outcome of the experience? A study by John Falk and colleagues conducted with children's field trips to the National Zoo in Washington, D.C., provides some useful insights.[16] The study explored the importance of different kinds of "advance organizers" on children's learning, behavior during, and attitudes toward a zoo field trip. Advance organizers provide learners with conceptual information to help structure their subsequent learning of a topic. (C. G. Screven refers to them as "pre-organizers.")[17]

Based on Falk's and others' studies, Falk and John Balling came to believe that previous experiences—not just intellectual, but also social and physical—significantly affect the visitor's museum experience. Some of the effect of previous experiences was subconscious, but much was conscious. A conspicuous manifestation of the conscious social, personal, and physical experiences was the formation of a visit agenda.

Discussions with children revealed that they did not enter a field trip experience devoid of notions of what would or, more importantly, should occur. Most children, even quite young children, could articulate what they anticipated happening on the trip. Furthermore, most children would also express what they *hoped* would occur on the field trip. Their expectations included a long bus ride, a day away from school, a special lunch (purchased or brought from home), and some kind of "lesson" taught by an "expert."

For a visit to a museum, the children's hopes included seeing favorite exhibits. "Favorite" was determined either by their own past experiences, or those of other people they knew, including parents and friends. Virtually every museum possesses a reputation for certain exhibits which in a very real sense precedes the museum and may well affect the visitor's behavior once inside. Children also relished the possibility of buying something at the gift shop, and most had brought a small amount of money for that purpose.

Children thus begin a field trip with two agendas. One is very child-centered—seeing favorite exhibits, buying something at the gift shop, having fun on the bus, and getting a day off from the normal school routine. The other agenda is similar to that of the school and museum—meeting museum experts and learning about some of the museum's offerings.

Falk and Balling believed that the interaction between the children's "ideal" experience (as expressed by their hopes and expectations) and their "real" experience (as expressed in the events as they actually occurred) should measurably affect the outcome of the trip. Specifically, the study was designed to investigate how manipulating these expectations, or agendas, before a visit affected children's learning and behavior.

More than 900 children were taken on a total of thirty-three school field trips to the zoo.[18]* Before the trip they participated in an "orientation" session. Three different types of orientation were designed, representing three different approaches. All three included a slide presentation, an individualized game to be done at the student's seat, and a poster that could be hung in the classroom. The first two types of orientation were designed to influence what was called the children's school agenda, and the third was designed to accommodate the child's agenda.

The first orientation type was cognitive. The researchers described the concepts that would be discussed on the visit to the zoo and talked about what students might learn. This is typical of the kind of orientation session museums offer before field trips. The researchers also had a slide presentation showing the specific animals to be studied, a discussion of mammal adaptations to aquatic environments, a work sheet emphasizing key concepts such as streamlining and adaptations for breathing, and an aquatic mammals poster.

The second type of orientation was based on "process skills." The researchers explained to the students that a zoo visit requires good observational skills and offered them some strategies for improving their ability to see things at the zoo. This is, in essence, the agenda of the zoo expert, who tells the children how the experts themselves behave at the

---

*The children were all fourth graders from communities within roughly a one-hour bus trip from Washington, D.C. Nearly all the children had been to the National Zoo before.

zoo. The slides, work sheet, and poster all emphasized observational skills.

The third type of orientation was child-centered, intended to set the children at ease about the trip by informing them about practical aspects of their agendas on the field trip. The researchers explained how they would get to the zoo, where they would park, and what they would do while at the zoo—what they would see, what they could buy, and what they would have for lunch. The slide presentation walked the children through the zoo visit. The work sheet and poster included a map of the zoo and familiar animals that they would see.

The children were divided in five groups. The three test groups described above were given a pre-test one month before the visit, a post-test within a week after the visit, and a second post-test three months after the visit. The tests measured concept learning, knowledge of setting, observational skills, and attitudes. These three groups were also observed during their visit. In addition to the three test groups, two control groups took both the pre-visit and post-visit tests: one that went on the field trip with no orientation session, and one (a "test-only" group) that had neither an orientation session nor a field trip.

The results of this study were informative and complex. The test-only control group did not show any significant learning. All groups that went on the field trip (including the "no orientation" control group) showed significant learning in the three areas of content, observational skills, and knowledge of setting. Moreover, as demonstrated by the second post-test, learning persisted over three months. In addition, based on attitudinal questions on the test, all groups showed significant positive changes in their attitudes toward animals in general and zoos in particular.

Notably, children who received two of the three types of orientation showed significantly higher learning than the control group that did not receive an orientation but went on the field trip. These two groups were those who received the cognitive orientation and those who received the child-centered orientation.

The child-centered orientation group showed significantly higher learning than any other group. Those students who were told where the bus would park and what was sold at the concession stands performed better on a cognitive test of zoo animals than did the group that was provided information on what cognitive facts and concepts were to be presented. The former group also showed significantly better observational skills than did those who were provided the observation-orientation session.

The researchers' explanation for this counter-intuitive finding was that every child on that field trip began with a personal agenda of what he hoped to see or do during that field trip. It may have been which gifts to buy, which kinds of food to eat, or which animals to see, or it may have been a particular curiosity about aquatic mammals, the theme of the field trip lesson. Regardless of the nature of a student's personal agenda, the previous knowledge that he would, or would not, be able to satisfy that agenda helped him "perform" better on the "lesson" part of the trip. Children who were not given the child-centered information went through the motions of the field trip but, presumably, were wondering the whole time: "Will I get a chance to see a panda?" or "What do they sell in the gift shop, and will I get a chance to buy anything with the dollar I brought?"

The behavioral observations made of these children during the field trip experience reinforced the paper and pencil measures.[19] The child-centered orientation group seemed more relaxed and attentive to the docent than did the other groups. It is probably significant that most of these children had visited the National Zoo before. Those who had not been briefed on this particular trip to the zoo were restless, as they knew from earlier experience what they wanted to see and do but were not sure they would be able to do so.

Although this study was conducted with nine- and ten-year-old children in a school field trip context, the findings may be generalizable to all museum visitors. Whether a visitor is nine or ninety, part of a school group, adult group, family, or by himself, he comes to a museum with the expectation of seeing certain things and of doing certain things.

These hopes and expectations vary from visitor to visitor; they derive from a variety of sources, but they are always there. Visitors to a museum have heard that they *must see* a certain painting, or they *must visit* a particular collection. They feel that, if they do not, no matter how wonderful the rest of the visit, it will somehow be incomplete.

The researchers conducted a follow-up to this study that sheds additional light on the importance of visitor expectations. At the conclusion of the first National Zoo study, they constructed a classroom lesson that permitted direct comparisons between the effectiveness of teaching a lesson in the classroom versus taking children on a field trip and teaching the lesson there. This is an issue of significant importance to museum practitioners. This study compared two groups of children who went to the zoo with a third group who did not, but who had learned about animals in the classroom.[20] The 102 children who had had classroom instruction were compared with 105 children who went to the zoo and were given a "Mammals that Swim" lesson while observing the four target animal species actively moving about their enclosures and with a third group of 97 children who went to the zoo and were given the "Mammals that Swim" lesson, but saw only two or three of the animals. In the third group, the lesson was presented in front of one of the enclosures, but, for a variety of reasons, the animals were absent.

Once again, the researchers used concept learning, as measured by pre- and post-tests, to evaluate the museum experience. The overall results showed that there were significant differences in concept learning among the three groups. All groups showed significant learning between pre-test and post-test, but the groups that went to the zoo showed significantly greater concept learning than the classroom group, and the group that saw all four animals showed significantly greater concept learning than the groups that went to the zoo but saw only two or three animals. The conclusion was not only that real-world or relevant contexts support and enhance concept learning, but that expectations figure prominently in this outcome. The researchers postulated that the children going to the zoo expected to see and learn about animals, whether they saw them all or not, and hence were more receptive to the information provided than were children who did not go to the zoo. Actually seeing all the animals was the most reinforcing learning condition, but the very act of going to the zoo was sufficient to enhance concept learning over classroom-bound peers.

Visitors to zoos expect to see animals. Visitors to history museums expect to see historical objects. Visitors to art museums expect to see art. These content-specific expectations seem not only to form a major part of the visitor's agenda for a visit but also appear to influence the outcomes of a visit.

Social Influences on the Agenda

Most visitors come to museums as part of a social group, which plays a major role in shaping their agendas. Adults elect to visit museums because they are accessible and safe, they facilitate positive social interactions, and they are educational for their children. Overall, many parents believe that museums provide excellent backdrops for family outings.

A pilot study on family groups at the National Zoo, designed to build upon the study of school groups described earlier, suggested that family enjoyment was the overwhelming criterion for visiting the zoo, and that whether or not the family enjoyed the visit influenced the family's perception of the value of the trip.[21] Preliminary results from this study suggested that the zoo's efforts to give visitors information on family activities and the whereabouts of rest rooms and exhibits of particular interest to families greatly enhanced the visitors' perceptions of the quality of their visits. Attention to the visitors' social agenda is one way that museums can enhance the overall cognitive and social quality of a museum visit for families.

Family visitors to museums constitute a significant percentage of all visitors to museums, but they are a diverse population. Because family visitors often span several generations, they have diverse expectations and experiences. This diversity applies not only in the cognitive realm, but also in the social realm. Adult family members come to the museum with social expectations that are different from those of their children. Even among adult members of the family group, expectations may not be the same. We found that some parents were primarily concerned with influencing their children's educational experiences; others were equally or more concerned with their own educational experiences.[22] These differences appeared both within and between family groups.

In a series of interviews conducted with children and their parents before and after their museum visits, a number of interesting differences emerged among the generations.[23] Many of the adults interviewed expressed the expectations and concerns Rosenfeld and others have predicted; these concerns were primarily social.[24] Children, by and large, did not express concerns about the social aspects of the visit. Children who visited museums as part of family groups were much more similar to children on school field trips than they were to adults on family trips. Specifically, the children's interests and concerns centered around favorite exhibits, the gift shop, and food.

Although these data are still too preliminary to warrant generalizations, the pattern appears to be that pre-visit expectations closely parallel post-visit outcomes. That means that the structure of the visitor's agenda determines, to a large extent, the museum experience eventually recalled.

Adults, whether alone or in groups, have expectations very different from those of family groups. Adults with their families are typically preoccupied with their children; adults in other groups, however, are typically preoccupied with the nature and content of exhibits. Their expectations center more around what they will see at the museum than their social group.

Certain adult visitors to museums, however, have social agendas similar to parent visitors, except that the objects of social concern are other adults. Some of these adults use museums as places to take visiting relatives. Others use museums as places to go on a date. Still others use museums as places to meet other adults. These adult visitors have a primarily social agenda for the visit. And although the dynamics will be different between two adults and between an adult and a child, the results may not be very different. For example, no matter what the visitor group, if one member of the group is unhappy or bored, the visit is likely to be cut short, because the needs, comfort, and happiness of all group members are pivotal to the success of the visit.

Adults who visit museums frequently are more likely than occasional visitors to come without children and outside of organized groups.[25] They may visit a museum between four and forty times in a year. Their agendas are honed by direct personal experience and knowledge. Because these visitors are so well informed, their expectations are closely tied to the actual offerings of the museum. An effective "feedback loop" has been created by recurrent visits.

Informed expectations led to a close fit between the visitor's museum agenda and the actual museum experience. This, in turn, leads to a positive, reinforcing attitude about museums. These visitors want to replicate the museum experience, which produces an informed expectation of what will happen on the next visit, and so on. Traditional formats that the museum uses to inform the public, such as announcements of special exhibits or direct mail, are sufficient to keep this audience informed and their expectations realistic.

The visitor's personal context is perhaps the single greatest influence on the visitor's museum experience, and perhaps the most important manifestation of the personal context is the visitor's agenda. It is important for museum professionals to understand the significance of visitors' agendas, and to recognize that they can be manipulated by the museum. Indeed, manipulation of the visitor's agenda is fundamental to the museum's ability to create a successful museum experience.

SECTION II
During the Visit

3.
The Social Context: Groups in the Museum

Because most people elect to come to the museum as part of a social group, a large part of their attention in museums is devoted to the people with whom they arrive. Studies show that a great deal of the time and energy family visitors expend during a museum visit is invested in social dynamics.[1] As Rosenfeld stated, museums are, first and foremost, social environments, especially for family groups.[2]

Most of the research on the museum social context has focused on families. Consequently, most of our discussion here is family-oriented. Little research has been conducted on the social dynamics of groups other than families—a significant deficiency in the research literature, as museums provide a social environment for all types of groups.

Children visiting as part of organized school groups arrive at museum settings with social agendas that can powerfully influence their museum experience. As observed by Lois Silverman, adult groups also bring their own social agendas.[3] The museum environment itself provides a social context for the visitor; the staff and volunteers who work with groups are a part of that social context, as are other museum visitors with whom a group might interact. There is even anecdotal evidence to suggest that some visitors go to museums specifically to meet others (S. Taylor, personal communication, 1991). All of these social interactions play a role in shaping the museum visit.

Family Visitors

A growing body of research has provided useful insights into the reasons families visit museums and what they do while they are there.[4] Robert Lakota was one of the first investigators to highlight the differences in behavior between family groups and adult groups.[5] In a 1975 study at the National Museum of Natural History, Washington, D.C., Lakota compared adult/child groups with all-adult groups and described their behavior. Lakota observed a stable pattern of interaction within families. He observed that adults selected a hall or exhibit to be viewed, based apparently on their familiarity with the subject matter. Once the adults had selected the hall or exhibit, the child determined the level of interaction.

Lakota investigated the attraction of visitors to exhibits and how long they stayed at exhibits. For adult groups, both attracting and holding powers of exhibits were important, whereas only attracting power was important for adult/child groups. Once attracted to a particular exhibit, families remained, interacted with the exhibit, and then moved on; there was little variation in the time they spent at each exhibit.

In her study at the Lawrence Hall of Science in Berkeley and the Exploratorium in San Francisco, Judy Diamond documented the influence of children on the viewing behavior of family groups.[6] One finding was that most families did not read participatory exhibit instructions before they interacted with them; first they tried to understand by trial and error and discussing results among themselves; they read the instructions only if after discussion they still did not understand the exhibit.

Diamond also observed, in these science museums, distinctive patterns of interaction and exploration between parents and children. Children were significantly more likely than parents to manipulate exhibits; parents were much more likely to look at graphics and read labels. These findings are supported in studies by John J. Koran, Jr., and colleagues which found that children were much more likely to touch and interact with a hands-on exhibit than adults.[7] These researchers suggested that novelty and curiosity were more likely to be factors in the behavior of children than in that of adults, because adults were often already familiar with many of the stimuli children found novel. They also suggested that children interact more readily because they have not been as socialized "not to touch" in museums as have adults.

Rosenfeld conducted a study in which he analyzed family group behavior in the San Francisco Zoo and in a mini-zoo at the Lawrence Hall of Science at Berkeley.[8] He found that families came to the zoo with a range of social agendas, such as spending time together or sharing a meal, that were as important as viewing the exhibits. Rosenfeld found that successful exhibits in both zoos, as measured either by length of time spent looking at exhibits or the social interaction they elicited, required interaction among animals or between animals and people. Other researchers support this finding.[9] Rosenfeld also observed that parents seemed to use their children as a reason to visit museums. The children's presence somehow sanctioned their visit, although it was often evident that parents were enjoying the social outing.

Some research has focused on the different ways that mothers and fathers interact socially with children in museums.[10] The studies of Diamond and Rosenfeld, and that of Paulette McManus at the Natural History Museum in London, concluded that males tend to assume the dominant role in the family, often choosing which exhibits to view and engaging their sons in conversations about exhibits, while females tend to deal with issues such as tying children's shoes or checking to see who needs to use the restroom.[11] These studies, however, compared only mother/daughter interactions with father/son interactions. Lynn Dierking's research, which analyzed mother/daughter, mother/son, father/daughter, and father/son interactions, did not support these findings.[12] Her results suggested that fathers tended to interact similarly with sons and daughters; it was mothers who varied their behavior, tending to be more exhibit-focused with sons than with daughters. In order to be meaningful, these results need to be replicated, but they do suggest that the paternal and maternal relationships with children are perhaps less straightforward than originally thought.

Deborah Benton investigated the interactions of family group members with each other and with exhibits at four museums in the New York City area: the American Museum of Natural History, the Bronx Zoo, the Brooklyn Children's Museum, and the Metropolitan Museum of Art.[13] She found that the leadership style of the family tended to influence the time spent at exhibits. Families in which parents exerted some leadership spent less time on disciplinary issues and more time on exhibit-directed behavior.

Samuel Taylor studied the behavior and interests of visitors to the Steinhart Aquarium in San Francisco and found that families talked about what they knew from previous experiences, discussing the exhibits in terms of these experiences and memories.[14] As Taylor observed, these discussions provided parents with opportunities to reinforce their experiences and family history and to develop shared understanding among family members.

Karen Hensel's study of family behavior at the New York Aquarium incorporated the human communication theory of anthropologists, sociologists, and linguists, which analyzes communication patterns among people.[15] Families with children were found to interact, converse, and provide information to each other in recognizable patterns. Families moved through museums while conversing, and at exhibits were observed engaging in a predictable "exhibit watch."

Linda Snow–Dockser observed family behavior between mothers and young children in children's museums.[16] Her results suggested that play and social interaction constitute most of the activity one observes in families with young children in these settings.

Another study, by Taylor, describes family visitors to the American Museum of Natural History who received follow-up phone calls approximately one month after their visit in which they were asked if they had done anything similar to the visit since attending the museum.[17] Most families indicated that they had, citing as examples picnics to the lake or attending a sporting event, suggesting that their concept of the museum experience was general and included other kinds of social outings.

Although the studies described here have been conducted in diverse settings, using very different theoretical assumptions, there is significant convergence in their findings. All of the researchers conclude that the family museum experience is a social one and that social interaction plays a critical role in the experience.

It is also clear from the research that families have come to "do the museum" and that, consequently, they read some labels, participate in some activities if available, and like to "learn" something new. Research data also indicate that family groups are attempting to be model museum visitors but that they are also frequently disoriented, overwhelmed by the quantity and level of material, and desperately trying to personalize the information they are processing, all within the context of the social interaction of the group.[18]

Social interaction includes the questions and discussions generated by looking at exhibits and reading labels, as well as the conversations, glances, and touches that are totally unrelated to the museum. Falk and colleagues' data indicate that the typical family spends 15 to 20 percent of the duration of the visit interacting as a family, plus an additional 2 to 5 percent attending to people outside their own social group.[19] Collectively, these interactions make up what we call the social context.

The social nature of family visits is readily apparent from the following transcript of a family conversation recorded at mid-point (about twenty minutes) in a visit to a natural history museum.[20] Only the names have been changed.

> (A husband, wife, and two girls ages six and eight enter
> the museum's Hall of Mammals. They walk over to a
> case display of "Cats of the World," the two girls several
> steps ahead of their parents.)

"Oh!" exclaims Jenny, the younger girl. "Look at the lion." Mom and Dad stop to look at the lion. Meanwhile, Lisa, their older daughter, has already moved ahead to the display on "Canids [dog family] of the World."

Lisa says excitedly, "Mommy, Daddy, come here! Look at the wolves and foxes." Mom and Dad either don't hear Lisa, or choose not to hear her. At any rate, they do not look up. Lisa picks up a telephone and listens to the recorded message on canids.

Mom is still looking at the cats. "Look how big that lion is, Jenny. It looks just like Mrs. Wilson's cat, only bigger."

"That one over there is just like Bobby's cat," says Jenny, pointing to an African wild cat. Jenny notices the telephone and moves to pick it up.

"Who's Bobby?" asks Dad. Jenny does not pick up the phone, turning instead toward her father. "Bobby is in my class in school. For pet show and tell he brought in his cat. It looked just like that one," she says, turning back to the exhibit and pointing again to the African wild cat in the display. Turning again to her Dad, Jenny says, "Melissa brought in her guinea pigs. When can we get a guinea pig?"

Mom and Dad look at each other. Finally Dad says, "Maybe after Christmas, if both you and Lisa are good." At this point, he appears to realize that Lisa is not with them. Looking around, he sees Lisa, three exhibits away at a case full of large hoofed animals. He walks directly over to her. Mom and Jenny pause a few more seconds at the cats, then, holding hands, follow Dad over to Lisa.

Dad walks up to Lisa, and asks, "What are you looking at, Lisa?"

"What's this?" asks Lisa, pointing to an impala.

"I think it's an antelope," he says, searching for a label. "Oh, it's an impala. It comes from East Africa, and lives in a savanna. It says here . . ." As Dad looks up from the label, he sees that Lisa is now looking at another animal in the case.

"What's this one called, Daddy?" Lisa asks, pointing now to an eland.

"Let me see [pause]. That's an eland. It is the . . ."

"Look, Mommy, Jenny! There's a giraffe," Lisa shouts excitedly, pointing across the hall. Jenny and Lisa run over to the giraffe. Mom joins dad and, individually, they quickly scan the case full of antelopes and the adjacent case of rodents before joining their daughters.

"Let's stick together, girls," says Mom as she catches up to Lisa and Jenny. "Jenny, tuck in your shirt. You look like a hurricane struck you."

"Daddy, when are we going to eat?" asks Jenny as she tucks in her shirt. Lisa has begun to look at a film strip on the social behavior of giraffes. The film is activated by a button, which Lisa has pushed.

"In about fifteen to twenty minutes," says dad, looking at his watch.

"I need to go to the bathroom," says Lisa.

"Can you hold it until lunch? I don't know where the bathroom is," Mom says, looking around her, "but I'm sure there'll be one there. Can you hold it that long?"

"Uh-huh," says Lisa, nodding her head, but not enthusiastically.

Dad, meanwhile, has been studying the map of the museum. "I think we need to go downstairs," he says. Holding hands, the foursome leaves the Hall of Mammals.

This transcript demonstrates the highly interactive nature of the family museum experience. As this family moves through the gallery, one can see from their conversation not only the social context of the experience, but also the relationships among each family member's personal context and the effect of various factors in the physical context.

The conversation also demonstrates how families use museums to joke together, talk about where they are going to eat lunch, and compare objects to their own concrete experiences, as in: "It looks just like Mrs. Wilson's cat, but bigger!"

Moreover, the conversation demonstrates how much time families spend at a museum doing the routine tasks involved in being a family. Parents check to see if their children are hungry or need to use restrooms, and discipline them for inappropriate behavior. It appears that, no matter how compelling a museum exhibit for the adult, the needs and desires of the child invariably come first. An unhappy or hungry child will result in an early exit from the museum. A child's need to go to the restroom takes precedence over interest in an exhibit. Even a conversation about dinner, or what to wear to a social event the next day frequently takes precedence over conversations about exhibits.

As Hensel and Silverman suggested in their research, conversations are pivotal in a family's attempt to find shared meaning in exhibits. The conversation of the family in our example began by relating the cats on display with other cats in their experiences; they personalized the information contained in the exhibit. Although they began this conversation by discussing the lion, and then the African wild cat, the bulk of the conversation ultimately had little to do with those animals, but rather with the apparently longstanding issue of owning a family pet, a socially important issue for this family.

The African wild cat discussion also proved to be a useful way for Jenny's dad to learn more about her life at school. It also was a useful way for Jenny to bring up the issue of guinea pigs again—obviously something that she had been wanting to discuss. The African wild cat was used as a springboard for this family to address its social agenda. This is a commonly observed pattern of social behavior among families visiting museums.

The discussion stimulated by an object in a museum generally begins with ideas closely related to the object. As the conversation progresses, though, it may move to ideas only distantly related to the object, as we see in the sample conversation. Conversational interludes, moving in and out of topics pertinent to the ideas presented by exhibits, as opposed to the direct discussion of objects or exhibits themselves, occur throughout the course of the visit and, as noted earlier, last for roughly 15 to 20 percent of the family museum visit.[21]

McManus has reached similar conclusions after recording visitors' conversations and subjecting them to detailed linguistic analysis.[22] She observed that visitors' conversations were close and personal, but at the same time mediated by the labels on museum exhibits. All visitor groups she observed talked about topics described on the labels, and portions of the recorded conversations indicated that visitors felt that "someone was talking to them" through the exhibit. She concluded, however, that no label text would be attended to in its entirety, because family groups are, first and foremost, concerned with enjoying and maintaining social relationships with their companions.[23]

Another commonly observed behavior pattern among families on museum visits is what social psychologists refer to as "learning by observation," or "modeling." Modeling, fundamental to social interaction, is the ability to learn by copying the behavior of other members of one's society.[24] Modeling was demonstrated by the family conversation in the transcript above; at one point, Lisa picks up a telephone to listen to a recorded message and, without being told, Jenny does the same. Families also observe other families to determine appropriate behavior. The importance of modeling and its implications for museum settings are discussed further in Chapter 7.

What is clear after studying the research on family behavior in museums is that the museum provides a backdrop for the family's social interactions. Those interactions in turn play a critical role in shaping the museum visit.

School Field Trips

A significant percentage of nearly every museum's visitors are children on school field trips, and nearly every museum provides special programs and tours for them. Field trips provide social contexts significantly different from those of a family group. How do the experiences of children on field trips differ from those of children with families?

A clear, simple answer to this question is not available. What is known is that social interactions are important outcomes of school field trips.[25] In a comprehensive study of children's perceptions of field trips, Birney suggested that the structure of field trips (whether children were guided by museum staff or left to explore the museum relatively independently) produced measurable changes in learning and behavior.[26] Highly structured visits appeared to result in greater cognitive learning, but less structured visits appeared to produce more positive attitudes.

Evidence indicates that children on a guided school tour have a different museum experience from those on an unguided family visit.[27] Certainly, the social interactions of children in a large, common-age group would be different from those in a small, mixed-age group. Exactly how these social interactions differ, and what the resulting influences might be, though, is not clear.

Visitors in organized groups are often denied an opportunity to orient themselves to the space, and, where visitors are unfamiliar with the setting, this can have significant consequences.[28] In studies conducted both in the U.S. and India, Falk and colleagues concluded that the children were affected by the relative novelty of an informal learning situation. In other words, if the place children were going was extremely novel for them, such as a forested setting for inner-city children or a large multi-story museum filled with huge dinosaurs and elephants for young children of any background, the children demonstrated a great deal of anxiety and nervous behavior. An important behavior exhibited by children in these novel settings was affiliation (that is, social interaction) with their peers. Definite evidence of increased social interaction was recorded in circumstances that were highly novel.[29] The results were consistent with S. Schachter's hypothesis that affiliation can be a means of reducing anxiety.[30] Children in the novel settings could be seen chatting with their peers rather than attending to the instructor or the task at hand. In marked contrast, the same children attended to the instructor and performed the tasks assigned them when they were in the less novel environment of their own school yard. In novel situations, the presence of peers was a comfort to the children. If the children had been part of a family group, it could be assumed that they would affiliate with other family members.

These observations of children focused on how their interactions affected their levels of anxiety, not on how social mediation affected other aspects of behavior such as learning. In a study conducted at Sturbridge Village, Massachusetts, Geoffrey Hayward concluded that peer influences were extremely important during field trips, either hindering the potential for learning or enhancing it.[31] In Birney's study, children indicated that they: (1) enjoyed acquiring new information; (2) preferred to share the information with others, particularly peers, rather than listen to docents; (3) defined specific places and conditions in which they could best share this information; and (4) disliked certain social aspects of museums, such as crowding, that prevented the acquisition of information.[32]

Results from our research on recollections, in which we interviewed people and asked them to discuss their earliest museum memories, would suggest that the social context of school field trips is important; these memories may be retained for as long as fifteen to twenty years.[33] Most of the people interviewed whose earliest memories were of school field trips remembered social-context details such as whom they sat with on the bus, whether their parents accompanied them on the trip, and what their docent was like.

Peer interactions may be an important determinant of behavior and learning on school field trips; certainly, there is evidence in the school literature that cooperative learning experiences may enhance learning.[34] More research in this area is warranted.

Other Visitors

Museum visitors attend to other visitors in the setting as well as to their own social groups.[35] Research has demonstrated that social influences outside the immediate family or group also influence visitor behavior.[36] Beyond mere curiosity, visitors observe other visitors to gain information or knowledge, as revealed by two studies from the Florida Museum of Natural History in Gainesville.[37]

The first study demonstrated how modeling theory can be used to explain museum visitor behavior.[38] Museum staff had designed an exhibit on the geology and paleontology of Florida. At the beginning of this exhibit, in a site normally encountered mid-way through visitors' tours of the museum, was a special display of the rock cycle, including samples of rocks such as metamorphic, sedimentary, and igneous. This display, unlike all others encountered earlier in the museum, was a hands-on exhibit, meant to be touched by the visitor. When researchers watched visitors at this display, they discovered that most visitors did not touch the rocks in the exhibit, even though a small sign below it stated: "Hands-On Exhibit." Why didn't visitors touch the exhibit?

A number of factors prevented visitors from touching the display. It looked just like every other display, except that it lacked glass; hence, visitors were not sure that it was *meant* to be without glass. In fact, a number of visitors were seen tentatively testing the display to determine if it had glass or not. Once they determined that no glass existed, they stepped back and proceeded to treat the exhibit as they would any other hands-off exhibit. Many children came up to the exhibit and, in their naïveté, touched the rock. Parents quickly reprimanded them and told them that museums were places for "looking, but not touching." Not only did most visitors not see or read the sign below the exhibit, but many who did appeared not to understand the message. One person asked a researcher, "What does 'hands-on' mean?"

Further study was conducted to see if modeling could be used as a mechanism for positively changing the behavior of visitors. Investigators worked in pairs: one acted as an observer, the other as a positive role model. The role model approached the exhibit when visitors were numerous, stopped in front of the display, and began to touch the exhibit, acting as if he knew what he was doing. The observer consistently recorded that, after the role model left the display, parents no longer reprimanded children, and single adults now touched the rocks, whereas they had rarely done so before.

In a second, similar study conducted by Koran and colleagues at the same museum, modeling was also used to change visitor behavior positively.[39] The museum had designed an impressive walk-through facsimile of a Florida mesic hammock—an area of extremely rich flora and fauna that occurs at raised elevations in Florida, particularly in the Everglades. Placed at intervals along the raised boardwalk that traversed the hammock were headphones with taped messages. Each headphone contained a different message, but all headphones looked exactly the same. Most visitors entered the exhibit, picked up the nearest headphone, listened to the message, then walked through the rest of the exhibit. Presumably, experience, either in this museum or elsewhere, told them that all headphones would have the same taped message. Clearly, most visitors did not realize they could listen to different messages on different headphones.

Once again working in pairs, researchers were able to observe changes in visitors' behavior when the appropriate behavior was modeled for them. The role model would move from one headphone to another and exclaim loudly something like: "Oh! This one tells you something new!" Following this modeling sequence, visitors spontaneously changed their behavior.

Both of these studies demonstrate that visitors do pay attention to what other visitors in the museum are doing. One would assume that most first-time and occasional visitors would use modeling behavior, primarily during the orientation phase of the visit. Research seems to support this hypothesis. A small, but important, percentage of first-time and occasional adult family visitors' time is spent watching other families to see what they are doing, particularly at the beginning and end of the visit.[40]

Museums are social settings, and one of the things people like to do in social settings is "people watch."[41] Rosenfeld was one of the first investigators to document the importance of this behavior for museum-goers.[42] In his research at both the San Francisco Zoo and the Lawrence Hall of

Science, visitors stated that watching other visitors was something they did frequently during the visit and that it was important to their sense of satisfaction with the visit. Visitors did not have any explicit motivation for this activity other than curiosity about their fellow visitors. Watching other visitors seems to be a natural thing to do in these settings, and visitors enjoy it.

Although the data indicate that social interactions constitute only about 20 percent of a visitor's time, their significance may be greater than that figure suggests. Data on what visitors recall from their museum experiences many years later consistently indicate that the social aspects of a visit are rarely, if ever, forgotten[43] and, sometimes, what a visitor recollects are primarily the social aspects of the visit.

Whatever the group, what is important is that the museum experience is, in great part, shaped by the social context. The understanding of the information in the exhibits and the message taken away are very much the results of a group effort. Researchers have not, as yet, made great strides in using the group as a unit of analysis in studies of human behavior. Most of the data regarding families, for example, have focused on individuals within the family, rather on the group as a whole.

Taken together, the research reviewed here suggests that the social context strongly affects the visitor's physical context—the pathways taken in the museum as well as the exhibits and objects seen.

4.
The Physical Context:
Visitor Pathways

The visitor, armed with his agenda, has arrived at the museum. What happens now? Millions of people annually, at thousands of museums, reach this juncture. Given the unique nature of each visitor's personal and social contexts, one might predict totally random behavior. In fact, visitor behavior in museums appears to be anything but random. Studies of visitor behavior have been the major focus of museum research for nearly three-quarters of a century.

After all these years and hundreds of research studies, we know a great deal about how people behave while interacting with exhibits, but we do not have a complete picture of the visitor's experience because we lack a comprehensive model with which to study it. As stated earlier, the visitor's museum experience is not just the result of interactions with exhibits, but the sum of his constructed personal, social, and physical contexts. These contexts are not always of equal importance, nor are they always distinct and separable.

This chapter explores the interactions between the personal context and the physical context, and between the physical and social contexts of the museum. The physical and social contexts are extremely important in shaping the museum experience. Working together, the physical and social contexts tend to channel visitor behavior into a few predictable pathways.

Visitor Behavior

A variety of investigators have discovered that visitors deal with a museum environment in ways that appear independent of the content or design of the museum. One of the earliest generalizations was that most visitors changed their behavior over the course of their visit. In particular, visitors seemed to get tired as they proceeded. As originally described by Benjamin Gilman, "museum fatigue" refers to the decline in both the number of exhibits visitors look at and in the length of time visitors view each exhibit as their time in the museum passes.[1] Gilman proposed that physical exhaustion caused museum fatigue. By contrast, Edward Robinson suggested that psychological factors were of equal, if not greater, importance.[2] Robinson's student, Arthur Melton, observed that visitors spend more time in the first few halls they visit than in halls they visit later.[3] These findings have been verified by other investigators.[4]

Melton was the first to document the tendency of visitors to turn to the right upon entering a gallery; on average 75 percent followed this pattern.[5] A host of subsequent researchers have confirmed this tendency (of Americans, at least) to turn right inside the museum, regardless of exhibition content or design.[6] Melton also observed that exits have a tendency to "pull" visitors toward them; visitors will generally exit a gallery through the first door they encounter.[7]

The location of an exhibit can also influence visitor behavior. Exhibits located on the first floor of a museum are more heavily visited than exhibits on upper floors.[8] Exhibits near the entrance are more heavily viewed than exhibits located deeper within the museum.[9]

Preliminary evidence even suggests that the size of a museum directly affects visitor behavior.[10] Visitors to smaller museums spend more time looking at exhibits than do visitors to large museums. This may be because there are more distractions and things other than exhibits to look at in large museums, whereas, in a small museum, one is more confined, one can see almost everything, and one can find one's way more easily to see exhibits of interest.

The visitor's perception of the setting—in particular, the perceived novelty of the museum setting—also influences behavior. In a series of studies mentioned in the last chapter, Falk and colleagues documented the effect of placing children in unfamiliar settings.[11] For many children, museums are novel settings, and one reason museums are popular field trip destinations is that they *are* novel.

In Falk's studies, children were taken on field trips to settings where they either had some previous comparable experience or a total lack of comparable experience.[12] In one study, groups of children were taken on a field trip to a forested setting; the behavior and learning of children living near forested settings were compared with those of children living in unforested urban environments. The children were matched for age, race, sex, IQ, and grade in school. Despite the overall similarities between these groups of children, how they behaved and what they learned from the experience were significantly different. The results of this study prompted additional investigations and, in each study (whether in the U.S. or other countries), the conclusion was the same: Children are affected by the relative novelty of the learning situation.[13] In other words, if the setting is extremely novel, such as a forested setting for inner-city children, or a large, multi-story museum filled with dinosaurs and elephants for young children of any background, the children demonstrated a great deal of anxiety and nervous behavior. They always used their time adjusting to the new environment, but, invariably, they would not learn any new content as presented by a teacher or docent. In more familiar settings, children learned both about the setting and the content presented by an instructor.

How visitors allocate their time also appears to be strongly influenced by the physical context of the museum, no matter what kind of museum setting. A series of studies we conducted in natural history museums revealed strikingly consistent behavior among nearly all the 130 families observed.[14]

In these two studies, family groups were followed from the moment they entered the museum to the moment they left. The researcher who tracked the families identified one adult within each group on which to concentrate. Every five seconds, the researcher recorded the dominant focus of attention of that adult—for example, whether attention was directed to exhibits, members of their family, or other visitors. The attention patterns of adult members of family groups visiting both the National Museum of Natural History in Washington, D.C., and the Florida Museum of Natural History in Gainesville appeared to be consistent and relatively predictable. Although both museums are natural history museums, the two are very different in architecture, exhibit design, and visitor populations served. Based on the data from these two studies, but mindful of observations by Melton in art museums, L.C. Nielson and Diamond at science centers, and Taylor at an aquarium,[15] we reached the following generalizations. Visitors display great individual variety, in both the duration of their stay and their initial interests and knowledge; nevertheless, three "typical" patterns of behavior emerge, one each for first-time and occasional visitors, one for frequent visitors, and one for visitors in organized groups.

First-Time and Occasional Visitors The typical museum visit for these groups has four components: (1) orientation, (lasting three to ten minutes); (2) intensive looking, (lasting fifteen to forty minutes); (3) exhibit "cruising," (lasting twenty to forty-five minutes); and (4) leave-taking, (lasting three to ten minutes).

Most first-time and occasional visitors are initially disoriented; they spend the first few minutes in the museum determining what there is to see and in which direction to move. They stop, look around, and perhaps obtain a map. They try to make sense out of the maze of people, objects, and architecture awaiting them. As pointed out by Hayward and Mary Brydon-Miller, orientation experiences can have a significant impact not only on people's initial actions, but also on their ultimate satisfaction.[16]

Although almost every museum provides maps, considerable research (including at least two studies in museum settings) suggests that most people have difficulty reading maps.[17] For both adults and children, the first few minutes in the museum are visually, and often aurally, overwhelming.

Examining the museum plan on a map often increases, rather than reduces, visitors' confusion.

Right after arriving at the museum, visitors often consult with other members of their family or group, or seek information from a guard or information desk attendant. Very rarely, visitors will approach another visitor for directions.

First-time visitors frequently watch other visitors, probably using them as models to determine appropriate museum behavior.[18] Because American etiquette prohibits staring at other people, most adults do this with a series of subtle, rapid glances at other families or adults. They begin a generalized search of the museum environment for clues to which areas might interest them or to where an exhibit begins.

The direction the visitor takes depends upon the configuration of the museum and the interests of the visitor. In some museums, exhibits are designed so that visitors must begin at a designated spot. In others, the visitor may choose among a variety of possibly competing exhibits. Some visitors have a specific goal in mind, and set off directly for that goal. If all else fails, according to Melton and others, American visitors turn right and begin looking at whatever is there.

Significantly, though, in the first few minutes of a visit, the "naïve" visitor's attention is usually unfocused; once he decides where to begin, he focuses all his attention on the content of the exhibits. This period of intensive looking is quite consistent for all visitors, and can last forty-five minutes or more, but usually lasts less than thirty minutes. During this period, concentrated attention to exhibits lasts for several minutes, followed by moderately intense attention. Visitors appear to be reading labels conscientiously, observing items on display, and discussing the information they are gathering with their family or friends. They allocate relatively little attention during this time to general observations of the setting; between 60 to 80 percent of visitors' attention is focused on exhibited objects or labels or a discussion of them.

Most visitors, during the intense looking phase, seem to be trying to move systematically through an exhibit. Initially, visitors do not, by and large, appear to select specific objects or displays to view within the exhibits. They do not appear to allow personal interest or the attractiveness of the exhibit to play significant roles. Rather, visitors seem simply to start at what they perceive to be the beginning of an exhibition and work their way through to the end. For at least a brief time, visitors seem to look at everything. They are trying to do what they think they are supposed to do in a museum—look at exhibits and read labels. This period of focused attention on exhibits and labels is very finite.

The next phase, which we call "cruising," normally consumes the greatest portion of the first-time or occasional visitor's time in the museum. Usually around twenty to thirty minutes into the visit, some member of the group begins to tire. In family groups, it is usually the children who become fatigued first. Adults seem to realize, especially in larger museums, that intensive exhibit viewing will prevent them from seeing the entire museum. For many occasional and first-time visitors, seeing the entire museum is a significant part of their museum agenda. Perhaps because they realize that intensive viewing will prevent them from fulfilling this agenda, most visitor groups dramatically change their museum behavior twenty to thirty minutes into their visit.

In the cruising phase, attention to exhibits drops significantly. Visitors no longer actively read labels nor attend closely to most objects or exhibits. Instead they appear to skim the contents of exhibits. Occasionally, an artifact or label catches their attention or triggers a personal interest or curiosity, and they dwell longer and look more closely. Many visitors move rapidly through exhibition halls at this stage, seemingly searching for objects or displays that will interest them, rather than examining everything as they did in the preceding phase.

After the better part of an hour, feet are getting sore, legs are getting tired, the mind is becoming saturated, and perhaps the stomach is growling. "Museum fatigue" has long been recognized as an inescapable phenomenon. The hard floors, long hallways, and dearth of benches characteristic of many museums ultimately take their toll on even the hardiest visitor. Even museums without these characteristics induce fatigue.

Melton proposed that "object satiation" was the primary reason for museum fatigue.[19] He hypothesized that object satiation could be minimized by increasing the heterogeneity of the objects presented. To our knowledge, no empirical studies have been conducted to follow up on this hypothesis. Considerable anecdotal evidence exists to suggest that visual variety and stimulation play critical roles in reducing mental fatigue.[20] In addition, certain laboratory data support this contention.[21] The personal interests and experience of the visitor, though, may be equally important in determining fatigue.

During the third phase, visitors increasingly discuss issues such as hunger, the need to use restrooms, and the gift shop. Although earlier attention focused on exhibits, during this period visitors broaden their horizons to look at all aspects of the museum setting, including architecture, who else is visiting, and the cleanliness of the institution. Social groups enter at this point into discussions of topics totally unrelated to the museum. It is also during this phase that visitors become conscious of time. Most visitors arrive with a time agenda,[22] and they now check their watches to determine if time permits a visit to the gift shop, a stop for a bite to eat, or perhaps more time in the exhibition hall.

Eventually, visitors decide it is time to leave, perhaps because of fatigue, hunger, a feeling of having completed the visit or a combination of the three. During the leave-taking phase, visitors dramatically change their focus from things to people. They ignore even visually enticing exhibits and turn their attention away from the museum setting except to look for exit signs. Inter-group conversations increase dramatically; most center on issues such as where to go for lunch and what to do after getting home. Attention to people outside of the immediate social group also increases.

Frequent Visitors Like first-time and occasional visitors, experienced visitors also follow a predictable pattern of museum behavior. Instead of a four-phase pattern, however, frequent visitors are more likely to exhibit a two-phase pattern: (1) intensive looking and (2) leave-taking. Occasionally, even frequent visitors "cruise" the museum.

Frequent visitors have not been studied selectively or intensively, but the best evidence suggests that they spend on average the same amount of time in museums as do neophytes—one to two hours—although data from the National Museum of American History suggest that frequent visitors spend less time per visit than do other visitors.[23] There are significant qualitative differences, however, in the way frequent visitors use their time.[24] Experienced visitors are equally influenced by time constraints such as parking meters and other appointments, and are just as susceptible to museum fatigue. When they get hungry, they respond by making the same decisions as less experienced visitors, even though they have more information about choices of food establishments. The major differences between the patterns experienced visitors demonstrate and those that inexperienced visitors demonstrate are: (1) frequent visitors already know how to find what they are looking for in the museum when they arrive; (2) they do not feel compelled to see the museum in a single visit; consequently, they do relatively little, if any, cruising; and (3) they go directly to the part of the museum that interests them. The frequent visitor's pathway through the museum is substantially different from the first-time visitor's. It is far more efficient. The frequent visitor uses his general museum experience and particular museum "savvy" to eliminate the inefficient parts of a visit—the orientation and the exhibit cruising phases.

Organized Groups Organized groups demonstrate a separate set of behavior patterns in museums. Like other visitors, they are influenced by the setting in which they find themselves. Most organized groups are led through the museum by a volunteer or staff person, who may or may not be sensitive to the psychological needs and desires of the group. The way in which a guided visit is organized is the major determinant of its effect.

Organized groups, whether school children on field trips or senior citizens on a day outing, are generally guided through the museum in two phases: a long period of guided intensive looking, followed by a brief free period of exhibit cruising. The initial orientation phase is not normally part of a guided museum tour. This is not necessarily the way it should be, but often guides are not trained to be sensitive to visitors' needs. Research on orientation[25] is helping museum professionals to change orientation and visit activities to accommodate better the interests of organized groups.

As described in the previous chapter, social context has an important influence on the museum visit, but sometimes the physical and social contexts are not separable; rather, they work together to form a physical/social context.

Influence of the Physical/Social Context

Normally, people organize their lives by placing themselves in those physical settings that allow them to do what they want, when they want. Those interested in buying clothes or shoes go to a shopping center or mall. Those interested in finding a book go to a library or book store. Those interested in seeing art go to a museum or art gallery. People who go to museums place themselves in these settings to accomplish a variety of goals—recreational, social, educational, reverential, or a combination of these. Placing oneself in a particular setting is an active process. Some of what happens once one is in that setting is active, but much is passive and strongly influenced by the setting itself. For example, one may purposefully drive to a shopping mall, but once at the mall, one behaves in ways dictated by what is appropriate mall behavior: strolling, window shopping, people-watching, eating, and shopping.

In many everyday situations, behavior is both predictable and limited by physical and social norms and expectations. In the late 1940s, two psychologists at the University of Kansas, Roger Barker and Herbert Wright, proposed that the physical/social setting should be thought of as an "active, organized, self-regulating system" and not merely as a passive backdrop where people carry out actions that they freely choose. They proposed that a great deal of insight into human behavior could accrue if the physical/social environment were considered. They called these physical/social settings "behavior settings."[26]

Early in their careers, Barker and Wright tried to gain insights about behavior by taking detailed notes on the everyday lives of people. They spent long periods following children through the course of their days, copiously recording every conversation and behavior. After doing this with dozens of children, they realized that "the behaviors of children could be predicted more accurately from knowing the situations the children were in than from knowing individual characteristics of the children."[27] The records showed that each child's behavior over the course of a day varied with the immediate surroundings and that, in similar surroundings, different children behaved much the same. For example, a child moving from arithmetic class to recess changed from quiet, pensive behavior to loud, exuberant behavior. The child's behavior in the class was more like that of other students in the class than it was like his or her own behavior at recess. Although the children in Barker and Wright's studies did show variability (some squirmed more in their seats during class than others), they generally restricted their behavior to conform to the setting. Subsequent research by other investigators in numerous settings with both children and adults has shown this generalization to hold true.[28]

According to Barker and Wright, behavior settings are culturally determined. Within our culture, behavior is constrained in certain physical/social environments by accepted convention, not because of intrinsic biological force. When people go to the movies, for example, they know what to do: find a seat, face forward, and watch the screen. In this behavioral setting, it is considered acceptable to eat popcorn; it is also generally acceptable to leave trash on the floor of the theater, though in most other settings this behavior would be considered inappropriate. People in the movie theater do not feel coerced into this behavior; they just do it. Consequently, it is possible to predict, without knowing anything about the personal context of the people in a movie theater, some patterns of behavior they will probably exhibit. These patterns are both learned and modeled. People know how to behave in a movie theater if they have been going to movie theaters all of their lives. In other settings, when people are insecure about how to behave, they observe others to determine appropriate behavior. This is called "modeling."

Our research suggests that museums, like movie theaters, are "behavior settings."[29] Art, history, and natural history museums are institutions at which the public expects to find treasured objects of human or natural origin. In such museums, valuable, often priceless objects are exhibited behind glass and guarded night and day to ensure their safety. Visitors to such museums are expected to act reverentially, to look at, but not touch, the objects, keep their voices low, wear appropriate attire, and show respect for the collection.

By contrast, most science centers and children's museums, many modern exhibits in history and natural history museums, and some parks and nature centers encourage an active, hands-on approach to the exhibits. Visitors are expected to touch and physically interact with the objects; voices are often loud; laughter is encouraged; attire is casual; reverence for the exhibits is not encouraged; and knowledge of the artifacts is not considered necessary. Consequently, museums can be classified as "hands-on" or "hands-off" museums. As long as a museum is consistent in the way it presents its behavior setting, visitors have little difficulty in adjusting their behavior accordingly. When museums mix hands-on and hands-off settings, they risk causing considerable confusion in the visiting public.[30]

The trend for traditional hands-off museums to incorporate hands-on exhibits has gained momentum over the last two decades. It may be too early to tell how the public reacts to mixing settings, but John J. Koran, Jr., Mary Lou Koran, Dierking, and John Foster found that visitors to the Florida Museum of Natural History were confused by a hands-on exhibit discovered mid-way through a museum full of hands-off exhibits.[31] Despite signs urging them to touch, visitors were uncomfortable doing so, having been conditioned to expect objects in the museum to be untouchable.

Behavior settings represent one way to conceptualize how people are influenced by physical space. Proxemics, a sub-discipline of anthropology, is another approach to analyzing how people use physical space.[32] Research at the Milwaukee Public Museum, led by Stephen deBorhegyi, used this approach.[33] There are also a number of researchers who have investigated people's spatial ability and memory.[34] One common method to assess spatial memory is to have people reconstruct a "cognitive map" from memory, literally, the map within their heads. In preliminary research by Falk and Mary Budd Rowe, adults were asked to draw a floor plan of the Florida Museum of Natural History after a one-hour visit. The plan they drew one week after their visit was more accurate than the one drawn immediately after the visit. Seemingly, some form of mental consolidation of their cognitive maps had taken place.[35]

Despite the diversity of people who visit museums and the diversity of museums, themselves, as well as the variety of exhibit content and design, research on the physical context has demonstrated that most museum visitors behave in a fairly predictable manner, and that they will, in fact, spend a large percentage of their time attending to the exhibits and objects on display.

5.
The Physical Context: Exhibits and Labels

Although museum-goers have broad agendas, there is no denying the fact that most visitors come to museums specifically to see the objects on display and to read the labels in exhibits. Visitors spend most of their time looking at, and presumably thinking about, the objects and labels in exhibits, and leave with images of them. Even though the visitor's physical context can include a multitude of events or features, it is generally assumed that objects and labels have the greatest influence on the visitor's museum experience.

Visitors do not respond passively to exhibits and labels. Rather, they become actively involved in their immediate environment. Traditionally, museum professionals have failed to recognize that visitors create their own museum experience, and yet it is clear after watching visitors that this is what they do. As they move through museum spaces, visitors selectively look at and examine objects and labels in exhibits. They ask questions about what they see, hold discussions with each other, and attempt to personalize and make sense of what they see. The important aspect of their activity is that it is selective. Visitors choose, sometimes apparently randomly, what to focus on. The things they choose to examine are woven into their own museum experience. Each visitor's experience is different, because each brings his own personal and social contexts, because each is differently affected by the physical context, and because each makes different choices as to which aspects of that context to focus on. Savvy visitors may have an experience quite similar to that of the museum professional; less savvy visitors may have a different, but equally valid, experience.

Because most museum professionals fail to realize that visitors create their own experiences, exhibitions often seem to be designed under the assumption that visitors will stop, look, and absorb *all* the information presented. Research on museum visitors illuminates the flaws in this assumption.

A large part of museum visitor research and a considerable amount of thoughtful discourse have been directed toward issues of exhibition design techniques and the presentation and construction of labels.[1] Countless investigators have attempted to understand the interaction between visitors and museum exhibits, labels, and other aspects of what we call the interactive experience.

More than sixty years of research suggests that not all exhibits function as simply and efficiently as exhibit designers would wish. As early as the 1920s, Robinson and Melton were conducting research on how visitors allocated their time in front of exhibits. Their research, later reinforced by pioneers like Chandler Screven and Harris Shettel, helped fix in the museum community's mind the concept of exhibit "attracting power"—the ability of an exhibit to draw the attention of a visitor.[2] But this research found that, despite their best efforts, museum staffs and exhibit designers rarely succeeded in creating exhibits with consistent attracting power. Direct observation of the public revealed that some exhibits attracted a great deal of attention and some exhibits attracted little or no attention. It seemed that visitors were actively selecting which exhibits to view and which exhibits not to view. In essence, they were creating their own physical contexts.

This fact has concerned the museum community because many museums design exhibitions composed of groupings of cases or interactive displays that present a single, large, multi-faceted story or concept. Accordingly, many exhibitions are designed to be experienced in a sequence (e.g., chronological or hierarchical) to help the visitor absorb the information. Exhibit teams spend a great deal of time planning the sequencing of exhibitions. Each case or interactive display is designed to contribute a particular element to the exhibition, to convey an important piece of the larger story—like chapters in a book.

Despite great efforts on the part of design teams, it is well documented that many visitors do not view the exhibits in the intended order.[3] One group may start with the first case; skip two cases; look at an isolated case; move directly to another hall; then skip the remaining cases and move to another part of the museum entirely. Another group may follow a totally different path. Occasional visitors, in particular, are unlikely to follow the sequence, especially if they are thirty to forty minutes into their visit.[4]

In response, some museums have designed exhibitions that "force" visitors to follow the sequence. Such exhibitions are designed so that visitors must enter in one place and exit in another. Still, some visitors find a way to enter at the exit and exit at the entrance.[5] Even if they follow the sequence, they do not necessarily look at the displays in sequence. (M. Spock, personal communication, 1992.) Only when a docent or other museum staff member is there to guide them do all visitors follow the sequence. Left to their own devices, some will not view exhibits as intended.

Ironically, it is often the designers themselves who inadvertently undermine the sequential viewing of exhibits. Many designers, aware of the research, have concluded that every exhibit should possess maximum attracting power. Every exhibit vies for the visitor's attention.[6] When *every* exhibit is competing for the visitor's attention, the result is often an exhibition working at cross-purposes. The visitor's attention goes ricocheting around the exhibition hall like a pinball.

Visitors are often so overwhelmed by the abundance of sights, and frequently sounds, that they are compelled to be discriminating. Except for a brief period early in the visit, most visitors are drawn to exhibits that are either visually compelling or intrinsically interesting to them. At these exhibits, visitors do spend time reading labels and carefully observing objects. Visitors discriminate not only between exhibits, but also within exhibits.

The same research discussed earlier found that not only were visitors attracted to some exhibits more than to others but, once attracted, visitors were more engaged by some exhibits than by others.[7] Visitors stopped at some exhibits but then immediately moved on; other exhibits not only made them stop, but also made them stay and read labels, discuss them with their social group, or interact in another way. This characteristic is referred to in the literature as "holding power." Shettel also describes the teaching power of exhibits in terms of their ability to engage the visitor.[8] An exhibit may present a half-dozen options for interaction, but the visitor may choose only one or two. An exhibit case may contain dozens of artifacts, but most visitors will view only some of them and read just a few labels.[9] It all depends on what is most visually and intellectually compelling to the visitor. What captures the visitor's attention may be determined by an object's size, color, lighting, or shape; by the length or style of the label copy; or by the visitor's own criteria.[10]

Exhibit Labels

No topic has been more controversial in the museum field than that of whether or not visitors read exhibit labels. It has become one of the axioms of the museum world that visitors do not read labels. This is definitely not true. All visitors capable of reading read some labels; no visitor reads all labels.

A great deal of research concludes that visitors spend, on average, only a few seconds reading a particular label.[11] Because most labels cannot be read in a few seconds, it is usually concluded that the average visitor does not read labels. By and large, this conclusion was reached by watching visitors in front of exhibits and noting whether they read the labels or not. More than 90 percent of the visitors did not even bother to read the label at all; at best, they glanced at it for a couple of seconds.[12] A few visitors actually read the entire label. When the total time all visitors spent reading labels was summed and divided by the total number of visitors, the average reading time per label was in the range of ten seconds or less. Although these results suggest that visitors do not spend much time reading labels, there may be another interpretation.

Research in which visitors were followed during the entire course of the visit from entrance to exit, indicates that virtually all visitors read some labels, but no visitor reads all labels.[13] It also suggests that most label reading happens in the first twenty to thirty minutes of the visit. Data on visitor label reading could, therefore, have been influenced by the stage in the visit at which it was collected and which exhibits earlier researchers chose to observe.

McManus has also pointed out that reading behavior is an extremely difficult human behavior to observe.[14] Her data show that visitors who appeared not to be reading, or who did not have full attention and eyes fixed on text, actually included in their conversations verbatim segments of exhibit texts or paraphrases of the texts. She concluded, after re-analyzing her data, that more than eight out of ten groups of visitors studied had read the label texts at exhibits.

Another difficulty with the data on label reading is the use of an arithmetic mean to summarize the data. Under typical museum circumstances, the arithmetic mean or average is rarely a valid statistic. The mean is best used when the distribution is normal—falling within the familiar bell-shaped curve (see Figure 1). If museum label reading were normally distributed as in Figure 1, nearly all visitors would stop to read each label, some for a long time, some for a short time, and most for about eight or nine seconds. But that is not what happens. Visitors in front of any given label generally can be divided into two groups: (1) those that read most or all of the label, and (2) those that do not.

The distribution of museum label reading is almost always what is called "bimodal" (see Figure 2), in essence the combination of two normal distributions—those who read and those who don't. Calculating a single mean for this kind

FIG. 1
NORMAL DISTRIBUTION

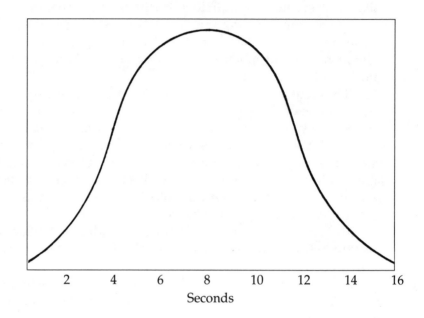

Number of Visitors

2   4   6   8   10   12   14   16

Seconds

FIG. 2
BI-MODAL DISTRIBUTION

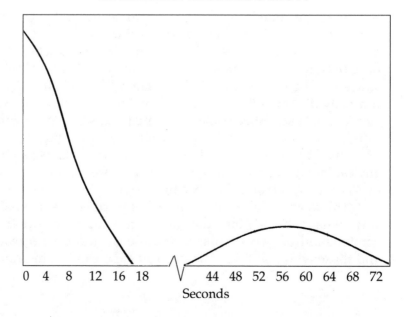

Number of Visitors

0   4   8   12   16   18   44   48   52   56   60   64   68   72

Seconds

of distribution leads to faulty conclusions. What is actually required is the calculation of two means, one for each of the two populations. Looking at Figure 2, we can see how this is true. Virtually no one spent eight or nine seconds reading the label; visitors spent either essentially no time or they spent nearly a minute. Almost any museum label or exhibit will yield this bimodal pattern of visitor attention: Most people do not read the labels, and some people read most, if not all, of them.

What this suggests is the commonsense proposition originally documented by Robert Bechtel: Either people enjoy the exhibit and spend time, or they do not and do not spend time.[15] An average, in this case, is really not useful information, as virtually no one spends the average amount of time at an exhibit.

It is easier to explain why some people do *not* read all labels than it is to explain why some do. The simplest explanation of why people do not read all labels is that it would be physically impossible. It would take an average adult reader days or weeks to read every label in even a medium-sized museum.[16] Frequent visitors already know this when they walk into the museum; inexperienced visitors learn this fact the hard way. Most occasional visitors begin their visit by looking at every object and reading every label. They very quickly learn that there is no future in this undertaking. The decision to stop reading every label occurs somewhere between five and fifteen minutes into the visit for typical inexperienced visitors.[17] After thirty to forty minutes, they become extremely selective about label reading. They read only those labels that satisfy a general curiosity or answer a specific question. Their personal time budget does not permit them to invest more than that.

Although most of this research was conducted at static displays, similar patterns are observed at participatory exhibits. Most visitors tend first to interact with the exhibit; only if they have trouble figuring out what to do, do they refer to labels.[18]

Besides time studies, what are other types of studies that have been conducted on labels? Borun and Maryanne

Miller have explored three aspects of label research: (1) studies that compare exhibits with and without labels; (2) studies of a variety of label contents; and (3) studies of a variety of label lengths.[19]

Most research on exhibits and labels has centered on the characteristics of the exhibit, such as lighting and color; whether or not labels are read; and the order in which visitors encounter the information in an exhibit. Researchers have tended to study exhibit watching in isolation from other experiences that visitors might be having, such as an enjoyable social experience. This approach, based on stimulus-response psychology, tends to ignore the roles of the personal and social contexts which, in our view, filter and shape the external variables of the physical context

The Visitor's Frame of Reference

Museums are novel environments, full of strange and wonderful things. Visitors come to museums to learn about these things and, of necessity, they rely upon their conceptual frameworks—their knowledge and experience—to understand what they encounter. They read labels either to confirm their own conceptual framework ("Oh, a lion is a cat!") or to determine an appropriate conceptual framework if their own proves inadequate. ("Oh, I guess an impala *is* an antelope.") This holds true for both occasional and frequent visitors. The main difference between them is that the frequent visitor's frame of reference, influenced by education, hobbies, and reading, is more likely to be similar to that of the museum's staff, while the occasional visitor's can be very dissimilar.

Observation of visitors examining information in exhibits shows that visitors try, often quite desperately, to relate what they are seeing to their own experiences.[20] Given that many exhibits are organized in a way that makes sense to a museum expert, but not necessarily to the general public, it can be difficult for the average visitor to understand the intended messages. One can observe this in families with young children, as parents try to relate what may be esoteric information to the concrete experiences of a six-year-old. Similar observations have also been made with adult groups.[21]

What happens when visitors first look at an exhibit or object on display is predictable. Often, one visitor says "What's that?" or "How does that work?" A parent, friend, or sibling often responds, and then (and only then) attempts to verify the response by reading the label. Diamond observed this "checking answers" behavior frequently.[22] In some situations, visitors do not realize that they do not know an answer, so they do not check their answer for accuracy. In other cases, the label does not contain the information the visitor was interested in anyway, so he has a choice of being honest and saying he doesn't know or making up an answer. Many visitors do the latter. Professionals worry a great deal about the misinformation they hear conveyed in their galleries; yet they may contribute to it by providing information that has little relevance to the visitor or within which implicit messages not familiar to the visitor are buried.

A good example of the implicit-explicit message can be observed by reviewing the transcript of the family conversation described in Chapter 3. The family, composed of a mother, a father, and their two daughters, ages six and eight, entered the Hall of Mammals after being in the museum for twenty minutes.

The mother and daughter related what they were seeing—the cats—to their own experiences. Recall that the mother compared the lion to Mrs. Wilson's cat. The daughter was capable of doing this on her own, as evidenced by her comparison of the African wild cat to Bobby's cat. Presumably, the purpose of the display was to show the similarities of members of the cat family; thus, we can deduce that the message was, at least in part, successfully conveyed.

The display that contained the impala and eland probably had a similar message to convey about the similarities among members of the antelope family. But a comparable message was not conveyed to this family. When questioned by one of his daughters, Dad initially used the term "antelope" to identify the animal in question, but corrected himself by saying, "Oh, it's an impala" after reading the museum label. Why was the cat exhibit a success and the antelope exhibit a failure at transmitting the museum's message that biologically related animals share common morphological characteristics? After all, from the museum's perspective, both exhibits were selected groupings of animals, complete with recorded interpretive messages, a label that identified the grouping by family, and individual labels that identified each specimen by name and habitat.

Apparently, all four members of this family dealt with the exhibits at the highest level of conceptual organization of which they were capable, determined by the mental constructs they brought with them to the museum. The family already possessed a mental construct for "cat" which allowed them to assign all the specimens in the cat family case to that construct. They related the specimens to their lives in concrete ways because they were familiar with cats.

Dad thought he possessed a framework for antelopes, but he was not totally confident of it. When asked a question, he gave his daughter an answer, probably the one she would remember, if she remembered any. But Dad did *not* have a reliable conceptual framework for the antelope as a taxonomic group that includes all bovids of a certain kind rather than just an individual species. The result was that Dad dealt with each specimen as a separate entity (e.g., impala, eland), rather than as part of the larger group, antelope. It appears that the museum's message—"All these things are antelopes and share morphological similarities"—was insufficiently explicit for the visitor to comprehend. A curator might consider the relationship so obvious that it would not warrant explanation. The message should have been more explicitly stated, for both the antelopes and the cats. Even though this family got the message as it pertained to cats, it might not be so obvious to the next group of visitors.

Experiencing Objects

As discussed earlier, visitors normally talk about the objects that they see, but only sometimes do they discuss the more abstract ideas presented.[23] Visitors look at a collection of objects and wonder: "What is it?" "Where does it come from?" "What is it used for?" "How much is it worth?" "What did it look like when it was new?" Rarely do they wonder: "How did this widget change the course of history?" "Why is this painting a landmark in abstract art?" "In what way do these examples illustrate the principles of conservation of momentum?" We would argue that most visitors, whether adults or children, deal with exhibits on a concrete level, rather than on an abstract level.

This is true not only of museum visitors, but of people in general. Most people deal with information, particularly new information, in a concrete, "nuts and bolts" way.[24] Although this approach to knowledge may be frustrating to subject-matter specialists, it is an important fact that must be recognized and accommodated. Museums, perhaps more than other educational institutions, are uniquely suited to capitalize on this capacity for humans to learn initially by assimilating concrete information.

Museums differ in one important way from all other learning settings. Museums are collections of things, some intrinsically valuable, others not. Objects are the essence of a museum. The AAM has defined a museum as "an organized and permanent non-profit institution, essentially educational or aesthetic in purpose, with professional staff which owns and utilizes tangible objects, cares for them and exhibits them to the public on some regular schedule." Although the AAM definition does not apply in some respects to many science centers, children's museums, and natural areas, the exhibition of things—whether science exhibits, animals, trees, or marshes—clearly separates museums from schools, books, libraries, magazines, television, theaters, and virtually all other institutionalized forms of learning. It matters little whether or not a museum's educational goals are congruent with those of other forms of learning. The fact that a museum chooses to reach its goals primarily by displaying three-dimensional objects, while the others invariably depend on words and two-dimensional pictures, distinguishes museums.

Writing about museum exhibits, B. Sweeny (cited in Neal, 1976) stated:

> A museum is the best device our culture has developed for the transmission of ideas to large numbers of people through the exhibition of genuine objects. This is the museum's strength. This is what it can do better than any other kind of institution yet devised. . . . like other kinds of institutions, the museum has both strengths and weaknesses; if it abandons its strong ability to exhibit genuine objects and moves toward the province of some other sort of institution, its success in transmitting its ideas inexorably decreases. . . . Failure threatens an exhibition with long labels simply because a museum is not the right device for the transmission of the written word. A museum is not a book.[25]

One might say that a museum is the best device we have developed through which to convey the concrete facts of reality to large numbers of people. Exhibits—whether of artifacts, science demonstrations, animal habitats, or paintings—allow people to see, touch, taste, feel, and hear real things from the real world.

Observation of visitors confirms this idea. Visitors devote most of their time to looking, touching, smelling, and listening, not to reading. Visitors tend to be very attentive to objects, and only occasionally attentive to labels. After the first few minutes, only those labels which hold the prospect of directly meeting the visitor's immediate informational needs will be read.

Nevertheless, museum exhibits are often designed to convey abstract notions; label copy often contains the minutiae of a topic, rather than big ideas. This is an admirable goal, but, at the same time, exhibits and labels would be more effective if they conveyed concrete information before introducing the visitor to an abstract idea. It is also critical, as previously discussed, that all messages be explicitly stated.

Expert versus Novice Experienced visitors take in more of the objects in a display than do inexperienced visitors. This is because people are able to perceive only a limited number of things at one time, regardless of their intelligence. What distinguishes people from each other is the way they group or, as cognitive psychologists say, "chunk" information. In a classic paper, G. A. Miller argued that the capacity of humans to recall information was limited by "the magic number seven plus or minus two."[26] The limit is not necessarily on the number of items that can be retained, but on the number of meaningful groupings, or chunks, of items. One person may look at a group of items on a desk and see a pen, a pencil, an eraser, a stapler, a tape dispenser, a blotter, and an ink well. She may not notice a paperweight. A second person may look at the same desk and see a "desk set" (pen, pencil, eraser, stapler, tape dispenser, blotter, and ink well) and a paperweight. The second person can recall seeing more things on the desk, despite mentally listing fewer things. The degree of their ability to chunk, which we all do, is one of the major differences between experts and novices in any given subject.

Accordingly, expert and novice museum visitors perceive exhibits in very different ways. Experienced visitors are able to take in much more of the contents of a display than are inexperienced visitors because they can chunk the contents in higher-order categories. Inexperienced visitors see a display with dozens of objects, but they focus on only a handful. The aim of the museum is presumably to help the visitor move from novice to expert. Exhibition developers and designers can, and do, use features such as color, lighting, groupings, placement relative to the visitor, and, of course, labels, to assist the visitor in chunking information, but the visitor's success will depend equally, or more, on previous experiences.

Two types of previous experience are probably important. The first is knowledge of exhibit content. Chunking information in a subject area that is new to a visitor is not an easy cognitive task. The visitor who already knows about

Chinese ceramics will find it much easier to deal with a case full of Chinese vases, regardless of exhibit design, than one who knows nothing of the subject. The museum must be able to assist the neophyte, but accept the limitations that a lack of previous knowledge will engender.

The second area of experience is knowledge of how to use a museum in order to gain information, described as "museum literacy," or what we have called "museum savvy."[27] The museum-savvy visitor knows how to use the cues that the exhibit designer provides to assemble the exhibited pieces in larger wholes. The experienced museum visitor can compensate for some lack of content knowledge by using museum knowledge as an organizing structure. Frequent museum visitors often possess both content and museum knowledge, while infrequent visitors possess neither.

The points we have made in this chapter apply to even the most well-designed exhibits, containing excellent labels, in museum settings conducive to visitor comfort and enjoyment. Unfortunately, not all exhibits are well designed, with well-written labels, and housed in ideal spaces. Many museums contain exhibits that are too high for children to view; with glare from glass that makes it impossible to view the contents of a case; with labels that are illegible; and with automated devices that do not function.

Even though exhibits and labels play a central role in the experience of museum visitors, many factors come into play in determining the effectiveness with which these educational devices transfer information to the visitor. Remember that exhibits represent but one aspect of the museum to the average visitor. This was brought home to us in the most charming way by an interaction we observed at the University of Florida's Florida Museum of Natural History. A boy of about five and his mother walked into the gift shop, at the boy's urging, before beginning their trek through the exhibits. The mother was very patient, but finally she said, "Joey, come on. Let's go out into the museum." Joey turned to her and, with that wonderfully quizzical tone and look that only a five-year-old can produce, said, "But, Mom, we *are* in the museum!" And he was right. The physical context he called the museum included the gift shop. His perspective is shared by most visitors.

The visitor's view is not reductionist, compartmentalizing the museum in intellectual disciplines or exhibit galleries. The visitor's perspective of the museum is, appropriately, that of a consumer of leisure-time activities. It therefore includes images of the gift shop, restaurants, and the friendliness of staff. We call this holistic view of the museum the "museum gestalt."*

---

*According to *Webster's Seventh New Collegiate Dictionary*, a "gestalt" is "a structure or configuration of physical, biological, or psychological phenomena so integrated as to constitute a functional unit with properties not derivable from its parts in summation."

6.
The Interplay of Contexts: The Museum as Gestalt

Ask a museum professional to describe a museum, and most likely he or she will describe the collections, the educational programs, or the institutional history. Ask the visitor, and likely as not he will mention none of these. Instead, visitors will say: "It's a nice place to take children to show them their heritage," or "The museum is a wonderful place to take out-of-town visitors. It's interesting, inexpensive, and fills up a day," or "The museum is a quiet place where I can escape from the work-a-day world."

Most museum curators, designers, directors, and educators would agree that these are reasonable descriptions of a museum. By the same token, museum-goers would not question that museums use their collections to do research or that institutional history is important. But in their fundamental approaches, visitors and museum professionals differ tremendously.

The visitor's perception of the museum is functional because he is a user, not a planner or insider. His view is not limited to an intellectual discipline or to individual exhibits or objects; rather, the visitor's perception is highly contextual, including the personal, physical, and social contexts. The visitor's experience must be seen as a whole, or gestalt.

The Museum as Experience

The museum experience includes feelings of adventure, of awe, of affiliation with loved ones or friends, and of seeing, perhaps touching, and learning about new things.[1] These feelings tend to coalesce into a single experience perceived as a whole, but a whole much larger than generally recognized, or at least acknowledged, by the museum profession.

The experience starts with the decision to go to the museum. On the day of the visit, preparations have to be made, schedules determined, and suitable clothing and shoes selected. The experience includes the ride to the museum, perhaps finding a parking space, or navigating from the bus or subway stop. It involves locating the entrance and, often, climbing steps. The demeanor of the guards and whether or not the museum is crowded are part of the experience. The experience inside the museum involves the exhibits seen and the items purchased at the gift shop. Conversations with family or friends are important also. Lunch or a snack while at the museum may be part of the experience, as may a dinner table discussion later that night. The museum experience also includes post-visit memories, jogged by related words, events, or souvenirs, and the ways in which these memories influence post-visit experiences.

All of these form a single package in the minds of the visitor. They may be stored in different nooks and crannies of the memory, but they are somehow stored as an interconnected whole. Recollection of a single one of these incidents may be sufficient to allow recall of all of them.

Museum professionals want to know what visitors have learned, but have traditionally used a narrow definition of learning. They examine what visitors have learned from exhibits and labels, for example, which is an important aspect of the museum experience, but only one aspect. Museum professionals have neglected some of the less obvious aspects of the visitor's experience.

Getting to the Museum

Most museum visitors do not live within walking distance of museums, which are often located in downtown sections of cities. Most visitors drive cars or use public transportation; those who live close enough to reach the museum by foot, bus, or subway are generally not frequent users of the museum.[2]

Yet it is a rare museum that devotes as much interest and concern to the parking situation as it does to the exhibits. This is unfortunate, because ease of access and availability of parking may determine visitor attendance as much, if not more, than the nature and quality of the museum's collections.[3] More than half the visitors to the Philadelphia Zoo rated ease of weekend parking as an important issue.[4] The same visitors also expressed concern for the safety of their cars.[5]

It is not unusual for a visitor to spend twenty to thirty minutes looking for a parking spot. If it is a metered spot, the coins in hand or the limits of the parking meter may determine the length of the museum visit. Time will become a concern throughout this visitor's stay, and she will construct and adhere to a mental time budget. Often the length of stay has already been determined before the visitor enters the front door.[6] These constraints, needless to say, have absolutely nothing to do with the visitor's interest, attention span, stamina, or the quality of the museum's exhibits. The ease with which parking is secured, the proximity to the front of the museum, and the amount of time remaining in the time budget all contribute to the visitor's mental state upon entering the museum.

Most museum professionals are aware of the role that "museum fatigue" plays in the experience. Few, however, have seriously considered the fatigue associated with getting to the museum. If a visitor has to drive an hour, then face a long walk after parking, the length and enjoyment of the visit will already be significantly curtailed. Climbing stairs requires twice as much energy as walking on level ground.[7] Stairs can also hinder access to the museum for the elderly and disabled.

Along with the rise in social consciousness of the last few decades has come awareness of the subtle, and sometimes not so subtle, messages museums convey to the public in their physical and social contexts. For some, a museum that sits upon Olympian heights, surrounded by Greek

statuary and a seeming infinity of stairs, reaffirms the concept of museums as places of worship and reverence. In such
a setting, the museum appears appropriately austere and
classical. To others, such museums convey an aura of coloni-
alism and élitism (R. Sullivan, personal communication,
1991). Accordingly, they do not perceive these institutions
as welcoming environments. As one working-class person
said, reflecting on childhood visits to an art museum, "I used
to like those trips to the museum. You got a taste of what it's
like to be rich . . ." When asked why he didn't still go to the
art museum, he said, "It's not for me, for us . . . this place.
It's for people with money, or people who are going to get
money later on—the college kids."[8]

The presence or absence of stairs is not the only way
museums reinforce messages of who "belongs." Having
mounted the stairs, the first official the visitor is likely to
encounter in any museum is a guard. Those who feel comfortable in museums will be at ease in the presence of
guards, but for those who feel out of place or insecure,
guards can and do create anxieties. One individual expressed it this way: "Even the guards in the museum, they
come around the corner and they stare at you. My father said
he wanted to go up to one of them and tell him to get away,
because we weren't going to steal anything, and the more
he treated us as if we were there to cause trouble, the more
my dad wanted to go and punch him in the nose. But we
left the room where he was stationed, and finally we got to
another part of the museum out of his reach. Then Dad took
us near and said we really shouldn't be angry at the guard,
because he was just taking orders, and trying to keep the
museum the way the people who own it want him to. When
my sister asked who those people are, Dad said he didn't
know."[9]

Every museum visitor is affected by museum guards,
no matter how experienced the visitor or how much a part
of the establishment the guards seem to be. Guards come in
all shapes and sizes, in all forms of dress, and in a variety of
dispositions. Without saying a word, guards communicate

to the visitor the nature of the institution. For example, young, alert, military-style guards put the visitor on notice that this is a place where security is important. A quick glance up at revolving video cameras confirms this suspicion. Visitors to such a museum may never feel totally relaxed. They may look around to see who is watching them before sitting; they may become extremely vigilant of their children to make sure they don't touch exhibits. Inexperienced visitors will be particularly cautious about their behavior.

How a guard is dressed is not the only impression he conveys. How he responds in word and gesture to the visitor during those first few minutes of the visit is critical. In many institutions, the guard will take or inspect the visitor's admission ticket or inspect parcels and instruct the visitor to check items at the cloak room. Even if such interactions do not occur, many people will approach the guard to ask general questions. The tenor of the visit can be influenced by the demeanor of the guard. In many cases, encounters with the guards are the fine tuning on the behavior-setting dial. The visitor's expectations are either reinforced or modified by these embodiments of the museum establishment. Like all first impressions, these shape attitudes that will be long-lasting and difficult to change.

Inside the Museum

Once past the guard, the visitor finds himself in the museum itself. Many museums are large, imposing buildings with high vaulted ceilings, large indoor pathways, and numerous rooms that may be hidden from the visitor at first glance. The architecture, objects, atmosphere, sights, and sounds all differ significantly from those visitors are used to finding in other settings. This is not necessarily good or bad, but it is important; it means that many visitors may feel intimidated in a museum. Modern shopping malls, by contrast, are designed to be of moderate, rather than extreme, novelty, because places of moderate novelty have been found to be exciting rather than intimidating.[10] Museum environments arouse curiosity, but also anxiety. As we noted

in Chapter 5, the uniqueness of the setting can inspire atten-
tiveness to the exhibits, or it can promote affiliation to the
exclusion of the exhibits, depending on the visitor's previous
experiences and the museum's ability to relate to them.[11]
Moreover, Americans have come to expect a high level of
cleanliness and upkeep; in one study of visitor satisfaction,
well-maintained facilities and clean, well-dressed guards
were the highest rated public concerns.[12] It is difficult to
generalize about the effect of museum architecture on visitors; much depends upon the specific size and design features of the museum.[13] However, even the smallest, most
human-scale museum is by definition novel and thus capable
of engendering feelings of anxiety.

Some museums make it easy for visitors to know where
they are and where they are going, and some museums
make it difficult. All visitors want to know where they are
and where they are going, and if they do not know when
they enter the museum, they will invariably spend the first
few minutes trying to find out.[14] For many visitors, the first
questions are: "How much does the ticket cost?" "Where are
the restrooms?" "Where do we start?" and "What time does
the museum close?"[15]

Almost all museums provide maps, but many visitors
find them only marginally useful. A map's usefulness may
be limited by poor design or visitors' inability to translate a
two-dimensional display into three-dimensional reality.[16]
Organizations like Disneyland have redesigned their maps
using perspective to simulate the third dimension. Most people navigate better by landmarks than they do by Cartesian
coordinates.[17] Maps that have landmarks drawn in relief so
that they more closely resemble what the visitor actually sees
facilitate orientation. Eventually, with or without guidance,
the visitor will venture off into the museum; however, if he
does not feel secure from the start, insecurity will diminish
the visit and he will not be caught up by the experience
because he is worried that he's missing something important
or that he's going to get lost.[18]

Most museums have an information desk, more often
than not staffed by volunteers. Like guards, volunteers

provide additional social context for visitors upon arrival and, like guards, they indicate by their attire, demeanor, and attitude whether the visitor is welcome or not. Along with guards, information desk volunteers may be the only museum staff that visitors encounter. Museum professionals should be alert to whether or not their volunteers are representative of the attitudes and knowledge the museum wishes to communicate.

Restrooms One of the questions most frequently asked of museum staff is: "Where are the restrooms?"[19] Museum staff may find it annoying, but it is not a trivial question for visitors. The museum that has only one set of restrooms, and those by the front door, invites visitors to leave early. Use of the restrooms is one of the most predictable events of a museum visit.

How do the restrooms enhance or diminish the visitor's experience? Are they easy to find? Are they clean and operational? Are both the men's and women's bathrooms designed to accommodate children and infants? If not, what message does this convey to the family visitor? In a study at the Philadelphia Zoo, two of the highest rated visitor concerns were "easy-to-find restrooms" and "clean restrooms."[20]

Smells can create strong, lasting memories.[21] If the smells of the restroom (or any other part of the museum) are particularly strong or unusual, they may become part of the memories visitors take home with them. The next time a visitor smells a comparable smell, good or bad, she will probably recall the museum visit.

Almost all visitors use the restrooms; museums can use this as an opportunity to exhibit the ideas or themes of the museum. The bathrooms at the National Museum of American History, for example, provide information on the history of toilets, a display so intriguing that it once led one of the authors by mistake into the restroom of the opposite sex!

Virtually every museum has a gift shop; many also have food services. One institution determined that 41 percent of all its visitors purchased souvenirs and 75 percent bought refreshments.[22] Museum professional staff tend to see the gift shop and eatery as revenue generators at best and necessary evils at worst. Normally, an administrator separate from the professional side of the museum oversees the operation of these establishments. Direct management is frequently subcontracted to firms not associated with the institution, and managers are rarely consulted when "content" decisions of the museum are made.

In rating the museum experience, the average visitor deems the quality of the gift shop and food service to be as important, if not more important, as the quality of the artifacts or exhibition design.[23] Moreover, many visitors do not discriminate clearly between the time they spend viewing objects and the time they spend in the gift shop. For visitors, walking around exhibit halls, visiting the gift shop, and eating at the food service are all part and parcel of the same event—the museum experience.

Many museum professionals do not understand this. If they did, more gift shop managers would be required to spend time talking to curators and educators, and vice versa. The U.S. Department of the Treasury, on the other hand, seems to understand the relationship between museum exhibitions and gift shops; the Internal Revenue Service requires a museum to sell only items that bear some educational relationship to its collections if it is to maintain its tax-exempt status as an educational institution.[24]

Most visitors make a connection between museum collections and gift selections and purchase items that will be suitable reminders of their museum experience. Souvenirs have unfortunately fallen into low esteem through indiscriminate proliferation of cheap objects. Yet a copy of an Egyptian relic or a postcard of a famous painting, which some may scorn as a "cheap imitation," may be the best device available to the visitor to evoke memories of his museum visit. In our research on what visitors recollect of their visits, we have found that many people distinctly remembered museum souvenirs they had purchased as many as twenty or more years earlier;[25] many still had the souvenir in their possession. Museum staff should recognize that souvenir purchasing can be a powerful part of the museum experience, and can help the visitor recall an exhibit or program long after leaving the museum.

If economic rather than educational priorities dominate the gift shop, its strength as an educational tool can be severely compromised. Any good business manager knows that the shop must contain at least some low-priced souvenirs. But the museum risks hurting its image if low prices mean selling poor reproductions or items only marginally related to the message the museum wishes to convey.

The museum that wishes to communicate accurate information to the public and facilitate positive memories must do so in the gift shop as well as in the galleries. Properly presented, the gift shop may be one of the best educational tools a museum possesses. Adherence to high standards in purchasing, even of low-cost items, can augment the educational agenda of the institution.

Some museums actively hawk wares outside an exhibition, sometimes at both the entrance and exit of a special exhibition. In extreme cases, visitors are forced to walk through a maze of gift items and self-guide audio tapes, complete with sales-pitching staffers, to gain access to the gallery. The impression that may result is that the museum arranged this exhibition to sell catalogues, calendars, and audio tapes rather than for educational or aesthetic purposes.

Gift shop items can be sold in ways that make the shop an extension of the exhibits. Some museums are experimenting with small shops scattered around the museum and related in theme to nearby exhibits. Not only may they be serving an educational function, but they may help visitors to prolong their visits by providing a place to relax and unwind from museum fatigue.

Food Food services also send messages to the public. What is the quality of the food? Is it expensive? Are the facilities clean and inviting? One can also imagine ways that museums could offer food related to the content of the exhibits. If the museum has a special exhibition on the French Impressionists, it could offer French food specials. The idea is to use the restaurant as a revenue generator, a public service, *and* an educational vehicle for the museum. During festivals or special events, museums often serve food related to exhibits, and it is always well received. The subject of museum food deserves further study. Like other steps in enhancing museum effectiveness, however, it requires advance planning and coordination among all museum staff.

Visitors' Attitudes

One of the most prevalent and unalterable attitudes museum visitors share is a belief in the value of preserving society's treasures. People think of museums as places where treasures, both physical and intellectual, are preserved and displayed for the public good. The visitor, upon entering a museum, in large part because of the expectation that great and important things are contained there, finds it awe-inspiring. In some museums, it is an awe of objects; in others, of the ideas presented. Museums are places where people can see and learn about things outside of their everyday lives—precious things; unusual things; things of great historical, cultural, or scientific import; things that inspire reverence. Graburn has described this reverential feeling as "the visitor's need for a personal experience with something higher, more sacred, and out-of-the-ordinary than home and work are able to supply."[26]

Watching visitors in many types of museums clearly reveals that most display a sense of awe. They speak in hushed tones, quietly wait their turn to look at exhibited objects, and respect the rights of others to have a turn. The museum experience can be as much an emotional as an intellectual experience. Visitors describe museums, and their collections, as "inspiring," "uplifting," "majestic," and "special."[27] For most visitors, feelings of reverence are subconscious. Some visitors, however, are able to articulate their reverential feelings. For example, one frequent museum visitor stated: "It's the creative spirit that you're seeing when you go to an art museum, or it's the recognition of history and achievement when you go to a history museum."[28]

For most visitors feelings of awe exist before the visit, are enhanced during the visit, and persist after the visit. They exist for the museum as a whole, rather than any particular exhibit or object, though certain exhibits or objects reinforce these feelings more than others. Most museums go out of their way to ensure that visitors not only enjoy and learn from their visit, but also leave with an appreciation of the intellectual and aesthetic significance of the things represented in the museum.

Researchers often find that visitors have great difficulty analyzing distinct aspects of their visit, even well-educated, savvy visitors. In one study at an art museum, visitors had great difficulty discussing the relationship between a traditional exhibit and the hourly live performances associated with it. It was clear from reading the texts of interviews with visitors that they had experienced the exhibit and performances as a whole.[29] When the researcher tried to rate the two components separately, many visitors seemed surprised by the question and were unable to do so.

Consistent evidence that visitors perceive their museum experiences as a gestalt was what led us to develop the Interactive Experience Model.[30] Although some visitors remember specific information on content, if questioned, most people's memories are consistently interconnected and contextually bound. The larger issue, whether these memories represent learning, is the subject of the next chapter.

SECTION III
The Museum Visit Remembered

7.
Museum Learning Defined

Traditionally, understanding the long-term effects of the museum experience has meant understanding museum "learning." Can we say that the museum experience is a learning experience? Although museum professionals have long considered education one of their major mandates and learning a major product, the AAM, in *Museums for a New Century*, set as a goal a better understanding of learning in informal settings, and subsequently reinforced this mandate in the report of its task force.[1]

Still, many museum professionals harbor doubts, reinforced by decades of museum learning research, which suggests that there is little or no direct evidence of learning in museums. The data suggest that adult visitors rarely demonstrate significant recall of facts and concepts encountered during museum visits.[2] The research on children visiting as part of school field trips is more equivocal, but many of the studies fail to show significant concept learning.[3] A few studies do, in fact, demonstrate visitor learning of facts and concepts during museum visits.[4]

Why does there seem to be so much confusion regarding the nature of learning in museum settings? Learning is a much used, much abused term, and our belief is that the confusion lies in the various ways learning is defined as well as in some of the underlying assumptions of traditional learning theory.

For many years, museum professionals have sought studies, workshops, and seminars on learning theory and psychology. Unfortunately, what many have found is a jungle of terminology and technical detail that in no way seems to inform practice. Experts in cognitive and developmental psychology have been consulted with the hope that their insights will enlighten the museum field; in general, they have not. The problem is due in great part to the conditions under which learning has been researched outside the museum field. Most learning theories were derived and tested in the laboratory under highly controlled conditions.

Many of these theories neglected the important roles that the personal, social, and physical contexts play in learning. This results in a biased perspective of the types of learning observed.

Much of what constitutes the body of traditional learning theory is important, but it is inadequate for our purposes. Traditional learning researchers are realizing that learning may be far more complex than previously considered. Such specialists as social cognition researcher William Damon and cognitive scientist John Seeley Brown have suggested that learning theory has neglected the social nature of learning and the role of motivation in learning. They have also raised concerns that so much of the learning research has been conducted under controlled laboratory conditions, with little connection to real-world learning and motivation.

The word "learning" comes with a great deal of baggage; some of it useful, much of it not. Despite a great deal of research and theorizing about learning, science has yet to devise a consistent, functional description of what learning is or how it functions.[5] Numerous competing theories and schools of thought on the subject exist, and whichever one subscribes to biases one's opinion of learning in museums.

Much of the confusion can also be attributed to the tendency to treat as synonyms the words "learning," "education," and "school." One manifestation of confusion is the misguided notion that learning is primarily the acquisition of *new* ideas, facts, or information, rather than the consolidation and slow, incremental growth of existing ideas and information. The importance of such consolidation is often not appreciated in schools. The direct application in museums of school-based assessment instruments and procedures has also been misguided, as many of these have had marginal utility in school settings, and certainly have little validity in museums.[6]

Failure to distinguish among learning, education, and schools causes confusion among the concepts of learning cognitive information (facts and concepts), learning affective information (attitudes, beliefs, and feelings), and learning psychomotor information (how to center clay on a potter's wheel or focus a microscope). Learning, as defined by many theorists, focuses only on learning cognitive information. This is unfortunate. Learning is strongly influenced by what we know and feel as well as by associated visual and tactile information. Learning is rarely so pure as not to represent an amalgamation of all three components.

Further confusion arises from the distinction made between formal and informal learning. Classrooms are considered formal learning settings; museums are considered informal learning settings. In the 1970s, when museum professionals sought to identify museums as unique learning environments, the formal/informal distinction seemed to make sense. This distinction has become largely counterproductive; one wonders what "formal" and "informal" refer to and whether the learning processes in these settings are somehow different, or whether the outcomes expected are different. Learning is learning. It is strongly influenced by physical settings, social interactions, and personal beliefs, knowledge, and attitudes. Learning can occur in classrooms, museums, homes, and shopping malls. The content and structure of the learning are determined by the three contexts described above. The terms "formal" and "informal" have little predictive value in relation to learning.

For purposes of evaluating learning in the museum setting, we need a broad definition of the term, encompassing the richness of experience occurring within museums and emphasizing long-lasting memories and relationships. We need to develop a comprehensive museum-centered model that embraces certain elements of mainstream learning theories, but that prescribes a much stronger role for the variables of motivation, beliefs, and attitudes of the personal context and for the influences of social and physical contexts.

Toward a General Definition of Learning

Museum visitors must somehow perceive information before they can store it in memory. Under normal conditions, people pay attention to things that interest them. Their interests are determined by experiences, knowledge, and feelings. This is a classic feedback loop: People learn best those things they already know about and that interest them, and people are interested in those things they learn best.

People often favor one kind of learning over another; for example, kinesthetic versus linguistic. The mind internalizes perceptions and builds mental structures (or schemata, in psychological parlance) composed of many-branching connections throughout the brain. Consequently, no two people perceive, store, and recall information in exactly the same way.

Learning is almost always socially mediated. Because humans are social organisms, they rarely acquire information in a social vacuum. People learn while talking to, listening to, and watching other people. They incorporate other people's ideas in their own; even feelings and physical actions are amalgamations forged during social contacts.

People learn within settings that are at once physical and psychological constructs. The light, the ambience, the "feel," and even the smell of an environment influence learning. These influences are often subconscious though sometimes very powerful—experiences that are the hardest to verbalize can be the easiest to recall. For this reason, the role of the physical context upon learning has been one of the most neglected aspects of learning.

Many factors combine to create perception and experience. When one reads a book, the words dominate one's consciousness. When people visit a museum, they look at the paintings or artifacts there. They give themselves up to the immediate experience, responding to the stimuli of the setting. Normally, they select these experiences from a desire to be there, do that, learn this. These desires usually spring from within, but occasionally are motivated from without. In either case, the experience perceived is a *constructed* reality.

Learning is an active process of assimilating information within the three contexts, and it requires accommodating new information in mental structures that enable it to be used later. All information so accommodated bears the stamps of the unique personal, social, and physical contexts.

Personal Context

Each person possesses a unique reservoir of experience and knowledge resulting from both genetic makeup and environment. Psychologists have only recently begun to appreciate just how different people are, in terms not only of their learning styles, but also of their genetic "intelligences," their motivations, and even in the way memories are chemically encoded within the brain.

Learning style is an important aspect of personal context. Howard Gardner has developed one theory of learning styles with important implications for museum educators.[7] His model proposes that people are born with the potential to develop a multiplicity of "intelligences," which can be added to the conventional logical and linguistic skills constituting I.Q. Gardner's model proposes seven intelligences in which each person has varying degrees of abilities.

1. *Linguistic intelligence,* seen in the highly verbal person who likes to write and read and who has a good memory for detail.
2. *Logical-mathematical intelligence,* seen in those who can conceptualize math problems quickly in their heads and who win at chess.
3. Those with *spatial intelligence* have good visual memory and can easily read maps, charts, and visual displays.
4. *Musical intelligence,* seen in those who play musical instruments, remember melodies, and need music to concentrate.

5. *Bodily/kinesthetic intelligence* exhibited in those who perform well in sports and crafts.
6. Those with *interpersonal intelligence* have many friends, like to socialize, and enjoy group games.
7. *Intrapersonal intelligence,* seen in those who are independent, like to work alone, and have initiative.

Gardner notes that schools focus on three of these: verbal, logical, and intrapersonal intelligence. He would encourage educators to help learners use as many of the intelligences as possible, recognizing that everyone will have strengths in more than one area, with one or two intelligences probably dominating. He is pursuing these ideas in other areas of the construction of knowledge.[8] Gardner's most recent book supports the contention that museums are important learning environments. He goes so far as to suggest that a more museum-like model for schools, one that includes content experts and apprenticeships with them, might be a better model for teaching and learning.[9]

Another learning model of importance to the museum field is Bernice McCarthy's 4MAT System.[10] Based on a Learning Style Inventory (LSI), developed by David Kolb at the Massachusetts Institute of Technology,[11] it identifies four learning styles or preferences that people have for perceiving and processing information: (1) concrete experience (feeling); (2) reflective observation (watching); (3) abstract conceptualization (thinking); and (4) active experimentation (doing). McCarthy's 4MAT System extends these ideas and postulates four types of learners: (1) the diverger, who integrates experience and answers the question, "Why?"; (2) the assimilator, who formulates concepts and answers the question, "What?"; (3) the converger, who practices and personalizes and answers the question, "How does this work?"; and (4) the accommodator, who integrates application and experience and answers the question, "What can this become?"[12]

The 4MAT System is based on the same experiential learning cycle articulated by Kolb and incorporates the same learning styles he identified. McCarthy added to each quadrant activities that address left-brain and right-brain dominance. She was concerned that teachers in classrooms reached only the assimilators, who responded best to the traditional teaching strategy of lecturing. In her work with museums, McCarthy has suggested that using this concept in the design of exhibits and programs can help ensure that the learning styles of all visitors are accommodated.

Gardner, Kolb, and McCarthy are only three of a growing body of researchers who take into account individual differences and learning style in their models of learning. Recognizing learning styles can enhance the museum professional's ability to understand and respond to the visitor's personal context.

Attitude is a part of the personal context often neglected in traditional views of learning, yet it is increasingly apparent that feelings, beliefs, and attitudes strongly influence learning. Many educators and psychologists use Benjamin Bloom's "taxonomy of educational objectives," which distinguishes among three domains of learning: (1) the affective, related to feelings, emotions, attitudes, and values; (2) the cognitive, related to remembering, combining, and synthesizing information; and (3) the psychomotor, related to muscular skills, manipulation, and coordination.[13] Restricting learning objectives to these distinct categories probably does not best reflect reality. There is probably more interplay among these domains in the learning process than is commonly accepted.

Mihalyi Czikszentmihalyi's and Eugene Rochberg-Halton's studies of the interactions between people and things document the feelings and meanings that people attach to various objects in their homes.[14] Research by experimental psychologist Gordon Bower has focused on the relationships between mood and memory. His studies indicate that the way a person feels during an experience becomes an integral part of his memory of that experience. Evoking that feeling or mood at a later time may trigger details of a memory associated with it.[15] Personal feelings, beliefs, and attitudes form much of the basis for motivation, a key ingredient in the museum learning process.

Motivation The role of motivation has been treated only superficially by traditional learning researchers other than the humanists. In the 1950s, due in great part to dissatisfaction with the prevailing behaviorist paradigm, Abraham Maslow and Carl Rogers began exploring motivation and the social aspects of learning.[16] This led to a theory of learning called humanism. Although extremely popular in the 1960s and 1970s, its effect on traditional learning theory was slight. We think this has been a major oversight, and for our purposes, three big ideas emerge from this research.

Maslow proposed that humans have a hierarchy of needs, which can be illustrated using a pyramid.[17] At the base of the pyramid are the basic needs—food, shelter, and water; at the top of the pyramid is the need to develop individuality. People learn at each level of the pyramid, but the need to learn those things one might learn in a museum normally occupies only the highest portion of the pyramid. Each higher need motivates a person only after the next lower need is satisfied. This notion has implications for learning in museums. For example, the apparent need for visitors to orient themselves before attending to exhibits makes sense within this framework, as does much of the social behavior of groups in the museum. The model suggests that visitors needing food or water or those preoccupied with a problem at home or work will find it difficult to focus on the content of the museum.

Two additional important ideas emerge from the work of Rogers: (1) A person's learning can only be facilitated, not taught directly; and (2) a person learns well only those things perceived to be conducive to the maintenance or enhancement of self.[18] Martin Maehr contends that motivation refers not only to "liking" a subject (the traditional way of defining it), but also to choices the learner makes as to what and how to learn, to persistence in a learning task, and to continued motivation.[19] Motivation can originate from external sources or from within the learner. Museums are free-choice learning environments for most visitors, so intrinsic motivation and its influences on learning should be of paramount importance.

This area has also been neglected by traditional learning theory, which has focused on extrinsic motivation.

Philosopher Monroe Beardsley lays out some principles for creating positive aesthetic experiences, which in his opinion are closely tied to intrinsic motivation.[20] Czikszentmihalyi and Rochberg-Halton have studied the role internal motivation plays in the learning process and have come to the conclusion that it is a far stronger influence than external motivation.[21] They have described three conditions critical to internal motivation: (1) The tasks must be equal to one's ability; (2) There must be clear goals for what will be learned; and (3) There must be clear feedback. "Every time a person gets involved in an activity for intrinsic reasons, and not in order to pass a test, or to get credit, it is because these conditions are present. Otherwise it is very difficult to get people to concentrate on something just because it is there."[22]

Czikszentmihalyi and Rochberg-Halton have examined the way experts in internally rewarding activities, like rock climbing and chess, describe their experiences. They found that "flow," a term frequently used by these experts to describe "deep involvement and effortless progression," is what seemed to motivate them to do things that have no reward other than the acts themselves. Among the rewards of "flow" are a sense of being freed from normal cares, a sense of being competent and in control of the situation, a sense of discovery, and a sense of personal enrichment. Marlene Chambers has suggested that we should regard experiences in museums as "varieties of flow experience" to gain perspective on how to create conditions that enhance the experiences.[23]

Clearly, in considering learning in the free-choice environments of museums, the interests and beliefs of the learner are fundamental. Jerome Bruner advanced the idea that learning, particularly discovery learning, is greatly facilitated by previous expectation that there would be something worth learning.[24] In the absence of motivation for learning, little learning occurred.

In an effort to move beyond learning theory, psychologists in this area have explored other terms, such as "meaning-making," or "sense-making," to describe the processes a person uses to personalize and assimilate information. Linda Graetz investigated the way visitors learned about art. She found that learning was closely linked with the personal connection—via experience, knowledge, and feelings—that visitors could establish with the art.[25] J. S. Brown suggested, in contrast to current models of motivation that assume forces outside the individual, that learners are naturally motivated to make sense of things; what sustains motivation is successful sense-making, providing opportunities for learners to question assumptions and explore alternative interpretations.[26]

Perception Regardless of intelligence or learning style, the issue of learning ultimately rests on perception and attention. When two visitors view the same painting, one might assume that their experiences are identical. Although the object is the same, it is highly unlikely that these two visitors will "see" (or perceive) the painting in the same way. It is understood that learning requires active perception, attention, and encoding, but it is not as well appreciated that these processes are unique for each person. The antecedents of this idea can be found in the research and writings of Kurt Lewin, whose "field theory" recognized that experience is an active process encompassing the *perceived* "life space" of the individual.[27]

The concept of chunking, presented in Chapter 5, provides a useful approach for understanding differences in visitor perception and for explaining differences between the perceptions of content experts and novices. Some of the classic research on chunking was done by comparing chess masters and amateurs.[28] The players were of comparable intelligence; each chess player could hold about seven or so bits of information in his head at once. The master, however, looked at the chess board and saw, based on extensive experience, a half-dozen or so groupings of chess pieces, each of which suggested possible strategies, each with known limitations. Thousands of hours of chess play and of experience with possible patterns and plays built schemata that enabled the expert to acquire increasingly rich chunks of information with decreasing effort. The chess novice saw too many pieces to keep track of at once, focused on a half-dozen, and with this information was able to map out only a limited strategy.[29]

Two important research studies have focused on the naïve notions or preconceptions that novices bring to museums. Melora McDermott, at the Denver Art Museum, tried to identify the nature of art novices' aesthetic experiences and to compare them with those of experts. She found both similarities and differences.[30] Likewise, Borun, at the Franklin Institute, investigated visitors' scientific understanding of gravity and motion and concluded that the concepts and beliefs visitors brought to their museum experience strongly influenced the way they perceived and interacted with the exhibits.[31]

Experiences and knowledge not only influence what a person is interested in looking at, but also his capacity to perceive it. In the research on chess playing, the expert was able not only to recall individual pieces, but the relationships between groupings of pieces as well. This was not the case for the novice.[32] Often, exhibit interpretation establishes complex relationships between objects and ideas. These relationships may be so well understood by the content experts designing the exhibit that they are not made explicit on the assumption that the visitor will understand them. Because most visitors are content novices, it is not surprising that such abstract presentations are often misunderstood or ignored.

Modes of perception also vary. As suggested by Gardner, some people perceive more efficiently visually, others more efficiently aurally, and still others by touch. Perception, therefore, can be seen as both active and selective, and unique to each person. That is why, in large measure, five people can walk around a museum together for an hour or two and come away with entirely different museum experiences.

One other aspect of perception merits discussion,

although it is poorly understood and little investigated. An important facet of the personal context is the visitor's perception of time —not necessarily in terms of minutes and hours, though this is sometimes important,[33] but the general appreciation of time spent reflected in expressions such as, "I was having so much fun, time flew by." Visitors can become either so engrossed in their immediate experience that they are oblivious to time, or so bored that they become hypersensitive to it. Bower's research has shown that mood directly affects memory.[34]

Processing and Memory What constitutes learning is the ability of an individual to internalize information and process it for later use. Daniel Cohen, a cognitive psychologist, points to the important role that researchers see memory playing in the learning process: "We've come to realize that memory is a large word, an umbrella term, for a whole range of processes that the brain uses to translate experience into ability."[35] All psychologists seem to agree that learning is related to the storage of information over time. Unless information is somehow processed and stored in the brain, it cannot be said to have been learned.[36]

Memory is an active process. Past experiences are connected to recent experiences. Memories are consolidated, or lost, over a relatively long period of time, in some cases in excess of two years.[37] For some memories, regular reinforcement is necessary to ensure consolidation with existing schemata and longevity; others, such as those of strong emotional experiences, may not require reinforcement.[38] In every way, memory emerges as an important ingredient in the phenomenon of learning. Learning and memory are closely linked;[39] not only cognitive information is encoded for memory, but affective and psychomotor experience as well.[40]

Retrieval and Transfer Information retrieval and transfer are the terms used by most psychologists to describe the basic attributes of learning—the ability to use information to solve problems, answer questions, recount a story, or recall a visual picture or steps to a dance. To be learned, information must be retrievable for later use.

Recollection, like perception and memory, is also an active, process and far more individualized than early research findings have suggested.[41] According to John Bransford, humans encode general, highly contextual messages.[42] This profound insight is a frequently neglected aspect of the learning process. If we can understand how information is contextualized and under what circumstances, we will be far closer to understanding the complexity of human learning.

With few exceptions, recall is rarely "photographic," but instead seems to be "impressionistic." The richness of the impressions recalled is a function of past, comparable experiences and the length and depth of exposure. Significant for our understanding of museum experiences, Bransford suggests that "quick" experiences that are preceded by few or no comparable experiences, tend to result in only "broad brush" recollections.[43]

Social Context

Social context also influences what and how we learn. Learning is a social activity, mediated mainly by small-group social interactions.[44] As Richard Chase points out, learning is a special type of social behavior and museums are a special kind of social institution for facilitating it.[45] Numerous anthropological studies have documented that social forms of education can be highly effective in teaching everything from concepts and facts to skills and attitudes.[46]

Lev Vygotsky, a developmental psychologist interested in the social foundations of cognition, developed a framework for understanding the role that social mediation plays in learning.[47] In Vygotsky's framework, when a group is confronted with a concept to teach or a problem to solve, the knowledge or skill of any one group member influences the roles every other group member will play in relation to one another. Knowledgeable group members support the learning of less knowledgeable members by providing "scaffolding," or support in the learning process. Scaffolding can take the form of questions, cues, or other learning supports.

Modeling is also a socially mediated form of learning that plays a significant role in museum learning. Most people are familiar with learning by modeling: it is generally accepted that it is easier to learn how to swing a baseball bat by watching someone who does it well than by reading a manual. Many of the social, emotional, and even intellectual abilities of humans are learned by modeling the behavior of other humans, rather than through oral instruction.[48] How do people learn to be parents? How do people learn appropriate behavior around other people? These are essential experiences that we learn nonverbally, by modeling other people.

In the museum setting, visitors can learn by modeling their own social group, other social groups, or museum staff and volunteers. Social types of learning are extremely important, and evidence suggests that they are also long term;[49] yet they are frequently overlooked in discussions of learning in museums. Social groups, and family groups in particular, are the primary learning environment for humans.[50]

Several studies further support the idea that families, and children in school groups, use museums as socially mediated learning environments.[51] Parents ask children questions; children ask parents questions; both point to particularly interesting objects and occasionally read labels. The kinds of ideas discussed most frequently among parents and children are generally concrete: "What is it?" "How big is it?" "Where did it come from?" "Is it real?" Discussion of abstract ideas and feelings, and generalizations about exhibits, do occur, but for most visitors, such conversations occur infrequently, and for some visitors, not at all. Nonetheless, questions are asked, ideas are transmitted, and it can be inferred that learning occurs.

There is also some evidence that families have different social learning styles. Dierking's research suggested that there might be a continuum of family learning styles, ranging from "collaborative learning" to "independent learning."[52] On one end of the continuum, collaborative-learning families arrive together and tend to stay together throughout the visit. Often, the parents direct the visit, asking questions of children and selecting the exhibits to be viewed. At the other end of the continuum are independent-learning families, who tend to split up, even when children are young, and who do not interact as much. These families view exhibits separately, checking back with each other occasionally to share what they have seen.

Teaching and learning take place in both kinds of families. In collaborative-learning families, family members learn not only about the contents of the museum, but also that museums are good places for families to learn together. In independent-learning families, children learn about the contents of the museum, that museums are interesting places, that people learn in different ways, and that parents like to learn independently as well. Similar styles of family learning have been independently observed by museum professionals working with families during parent/child workshops (H. Santini, personal communication, 1988).

Dierking noted that not all socially mediated learning is directly related to exhibits.[53] For example, the family visit to the Hall of Mammals gallery described in Chapters 3 and 5 provided opportunities for the children and parents to interact, exchange information, reinforce family history, and learn something new about each other. Further evidence is provided by Gene Gennaro and Patricia Heller, who documented that educational zoo programs that included both parents and children increased the scientific literacy of both and at the same time enhanced family bonds.[54]

The long-term consequences of socially mediated learning are not fully understood. We do know that individuals whose parents took them to museums as children and who found the experience pleasurable are much more likely to bring their own children to museums than are adults who did not go to museums themselves as children.[55] More research is needed on the role of the social context in learning.

Physical Context

All learning occurs within a physical context, and this contextual stamp ultimately becomes important in determining what information is perceived, how it is stored, and when and how it is recalled. Where one is has a tremendous impact on how, what, and how much one learns.[56] Museums use physical space in creative ways, so it is critical to learn more about the effects on learning of physical space and ambience.

The need to consider the importance of context in our understanding of learning has been emphasized by such diverse and renowned thinkers as J. B. Watson, the founder of behaviorism, Jean Piaget, a major figure in developmental psychology, and Ulric Neisser, a leading cognitive psychologist. In his 1974 presidential address to the American Psychological Association (APA), James Jenkins stated: "What is remembered in a given situation depends upon the physical and psychological context in which the event was experienced, the knowledge and skills that the subject brings to the context, the situation in which we are asking for evidence of remembering and the relation of what the subject remembers to what the experimenter demands . . . memory is not a box in a flow diagram."[57] In fact, Jenkins was suggesting that learning and memory are much more subjective than most investigators have been willing to admit. The connectionist school of cognitive psychology, the models of which are based on neural physiology and neural network studies, also support Jenkins' contention that learning and memory are subjective and contextually influenced.[58]

Although context has been considered an important factor in the learning process for the last ten years, there have been few efforts, other than those of Bransford, to study it systematically. Bransford began by couching written passages in different contexts. In a classic study, he had two groups read the same passage describing a house, then later recall information contained within the passages.[59] In one group, subjects were told to read the passage as though they were home buyers; the other group was told to read as though they were thieves. The two groups remembered very different aspects of the identical passage. The home buyers noted how many bedrooms and bathrooms there were; the thieves remembered where the windows and doors were located. Bransford has now begun research using interactive laser discs to simulate physical context more realistically.

Falk and colleagues investigated the importance of novel physical settings on children attending museums and nature centers as part of school field trip groups.[60] In all cases, the children's conceptual learning was affected by the physical context; in physical settings that were considered slightly novel, children's conceptual learning actually increased, while in physical settings considered very novel, less conceptual learning occurred. Learning about the setting, however, occurred equally in both situations.

Falk and Balling investigated the effects of physical setting on learning in a study in which children were given information about a zoo in both appropriate and inappropriate physical contexts—for example, at the zoo, next to the right animals, at the zoo, next to the wrong animals, and not at the zoo at all.[61] Children learned most when they were a part of the most appropriate physical context. The work of Barker and Wright extensively documents the role of the physical setting in influencing not just behavior, but learning as well.[62]

There is a growing body of evidence that physical context effects occur at various levels. At the micro-level, even such subtle details as the placement of a door handle or the number of control knobs on a device can significantly affect ability to cope with the environment.[63] At the macro-level, perception of physical spaces as, for example, open and friendly or dark and menacing influences one's sense of well-being and security, which in turn affects ability to learn.[64]

Learning is a continuous, active process of assimilating and accommodating information within social, physical, and psychological contexts. Learning involves more than mere assimilation of information; it requires the active accommodation of information in mental structures which permit its use at a later time. Learning should be viewed as a dynamic process occurring at the intersection of the three contexts defined in the Interactive Experience Model, with each instance of learning bearing a specific and individual contextual stamp.

Each experience has the potential to be incorporated in learning, but not every one is. It is probably impossible to determine which experiences will result in meaningful, long-term learning, and which experiences will not. Experiences that embody rich components of all three contexts, though, are most likely to be long-remembered. What we know about memory and learning strongly supports the contention that richness of experience and learning are highly correlated.

David Ausubel and colleagues defined "meaningful learning" as the linking of new information to existing concepts and principles in a learner's knowledge structure. The network of relationships formed during this process enables a learner to recall learned material after extended periods of time and apply the material to new situations or problems.[65] Within a museum context, meaningful learning might involve a visitor observing objects, reading labels, or talking with friends and family and, in doing so, accommodating new ideas or information into his existing knowledge structure. The information is highly contextualized by the personal, social, and physical contexts. The information becomes part of the visitor's permanent store of knowledge, available for use long after the museum visit has ended. This is the kind of learning we should be interested in studying.

Museums are excellent environments for meaningful learning because they offer rich, multi-sensory experiences. The proper presentation of ideas through tangible objects, particularly if they are interactive, is a powerful device for sense-making and, thus, understanding.

Let us now look at a line of research that reveals some initial evidence of the kinds of learning that actually occur in museums.

8.
Understanding the Museum Experience

Despite years of research on museum behavior and learning, the data that provide evidence of museum learning are limited and not always reliable. Recent psychological research, popularly known as recollection studies, has partially filled this vacuum.[1] These studies are normally non-experimental and often involve a small number of subjects; they are intended to reveal patterns and relationships rather than to prove or disprove a particular hypothesis. To date, the most significant result of recollection research has been the revelation of important aspects of long-term memory for museum experiences, including the contextual associations we believe are so important to learning. These studies provide a good point of departure for understanding the museum experience, although interpretations of their findings must be viewed with caution.

Over the past six years, investigators have interviewed almost 2,000 individuals about their museum experiences.[2] These interviews were conducted months and years after the museum visits. The lengths and styles of the interviews varied, but they recorded a wealth of recollections that reflect the influence of museum experiences on visitors. Following is the record of one of our interviews:

> "Oh, it must have been nearly forty years ago
> since I was at the Smithsonian. I went with my family—
> my father, mother, and older brother. I was eight or ten
> years old. We went as part of a family vacation.
> "I remember the museum. It was a massive

building, full of lots and lots of hallways and so many rooms. We also saw the Washington Monument and the Jefferson Memorial that day; we went to the Smithsonian last.

"I remember being sort of bored. We spent hours there looking at art and butterflies, and all that sort of thing, until late in the afternoon. My mother really wanted us to go but I didn't want to go. My mother was particularly interested in dresses—First Ladies' dresses, and other period gowns. My father just patiently watched. My brother was bored like I was.

"The thing I remember best was seeing the *Spirit of St. Louis*. It was suspended from the ceiling. I had heard about it in school, and I marveled at the history. I was really struck by the way it was designed, the fact that it had no forward windows. I had never realized that Lindbergh couldn't even see in front of him as he flew, that he was flying blind. I was also impressed by the scalloped effect of the metal. It was such a weird, special type of plane. I remember just how amazed I was by that plane."[3]

It is clear that this man had learned an important lesson about the history of aviation and developed a deeper admiration for Charles Lindbergh in the process. After forty years, it is amazing that he remembered anything at all. Or is it?

This interview did not proceed from preconceived notions of what memories are or what aspects of the museum experience are important. Rather, it was designed to facilitate recall without unduly biasing responses. The individual was not asked what he learned at the museum, or whether it was an educational experience; he was asked to recall everything that happened when he visited the museum. Although this line of research is still new to museum studies, patterns in visitors' long-term memories emerge that enable preliminary generalizations regarding learning to be made.

School Field Trips

One investigation of kindergarten children's recollections of a field trip to an archaeology museum was intended to determine if this trip would be recalled and distinguished from other trips taken during that year.[4] It focused on the linguistic details of the children's reports and found that they were significantly different.

Perhaps more interesting, these children were able, for more than a year, to recognize and pick out in order a series of six photographs taken on the day of the field trip. Moreover, "Although there was a loss of detail in the children's recall of the novel occurrence, the structure of the reports remained specific and the content was surprisingly accurate."

Unfortunately, this study gave little attention to the *content*, as opposed to the *form* of the children's recollections. In general, children had a much better recollection of what they did than where they went. In a follow-up study six years later, the children initially had little recall of this field trip, though with considerable cuing, all could remember some details.[5]

In a recent study, Inez Wolins intensively interviewed children of a New York City third-grade class on their recollections of school field trips. Over the course of two years, the teacher took her children on a total of twenty-nine field trips to seventeen different museums. Wolins was interested in the effects on recollection of the frequency of visits to a particular institution, the nature of presentations at the museum, preparation by the teacher before the visit, discussions after the visit, and previous trip experiences of the children.

Wolins found that children remembered: trips repeated to the same museum, trips linked to classroom activities, and trips in which a child had high personal involvement. Again, children recalled more accurately what they did on a trip than in which particular museum they were. Although recollections differed, based upon the type of presentation during the trip (for example, whether the presentation was a lecture, work sheet, or hands-on experience), the differences were not significant. Learning, as such, was not explicitly addressed in these studies, but it seems reasonable to infer that those field trips that were best recalled were most likely to result in learning.

In a recent study, we asked fourth graders, eighth graders, and college juniors and seniors to recall a field trip they took in early elementary school.[6] Ninety-eight percent of the 130 individuals asked were able to remember such a trip.* There were striking similarities in both form and content of recollections in all three age groups. Most recollections were personal, often representing intensely positive or negative experiences that occurred on the trip such as throwing up on the bus, making a new friend, being really bored or having fun, getting lost or muddy, and being excited about buying something in the gift shop. Students recollected a wealth of ancillary information about the trip, including whom they were with, how they got there, and, in a number of cases, what they were wearing. Although all interviews were conducted within a school or university setting, students had relatively few specific curricular or concept-based memories.

Casual Visitors

A group of nine science, natural history, and children's museums recently began a multi-year, collaborative effort to assess the ways their institutions influence the public over the long term.[7] As in other studies, indications are that knowledge of and experience with the exhibits, social involvement with the exhibit, and personal interest in the subject are all important features of long-term memories of specific exhibits.

We have also undertaken a series of studies of the extent and content of long-term museum memories.[8] The transcript quoted at the beginning of this chapter is an example of the data in the series. Another transcript of particular richness and interest, included as an Appendix, records the interviews of six family members interviewed a year after a visit to the Natural History Museum in London. The family members include two children, aged seven and eight, their

---

*The three people interviewed who could not recall a field trip were all adults.

mother, aunt, grandmother, and great-grandmother. Objectively, all members of the family had the same experience—a roughly ninety-minute visit to a natural history museum—but each recalled the event differently. Several themes that run through their six recollections are consistent with themes in the more than 200 interviews we have conducted, as well as with those of Robyn Fivush and colleagues and Wolins.[9] These patterns, we believe, are best explained by the Interactive Experience Model.

- All had personalized the museum visit. Most details recalled related directly to an interest or concern that existed *before* the museum visit.
- All could explain whom they were with and why.
- All could place the museum visit within a general geographical context. Nearly all referred to some aspect of the museum's physical context.
- Most could recall at least a few exhibits and some specific details about them, though none could recall everything he saw. In addition, nearly everyone remembered roughly how long he was in the museum and his mental state at the time, such as being bored or "hassled."

Personal Context

Every person we have interviewed has provided insights into his personal context. Each of the family members who had visited London's Natural History Museum, for example, told us of his or her particular interest—for one it was dinosaurs, for another, animals in general, and for yet another it was purchasing gifts and souvenirs.

The visitor who described his excitement at "seeing the *Spirit of St. Louis*" clearly learned something personally exciting about this moment in history. We know he came to the museum with some knowledge of the airplane, because he said, "I had heard about it in school." Seeing the plane made him reflect on something known and understand it in a new way: "I had never realized that Lindbergh couldn't even see in front of him as he flew, that he was flying blind." This insight could have been conveyed in a book, but, we would argue, this visitor probably understood it better because he had seen the real aircraft.

The reinforcement, consolidation, and reshaping of knowledge are critical aspects of the learning process. Too often, educators focus on introducing "new" knowledge. Most recent studies of learning strongly support the notion that knowledge is personally constructed and is always built on, and consolidated with, previous knowledge.[10] In fact, some evidence suggests that these processes may not even function as well if information is totally new.[11]

Moreover, all memories are embedded in the personal context. The museum visit is used as a personal marker for a host of events besides the experience itself. Ulrich Neisser has specifically addressed the kind of personal contextual memory evidenced in these kinds of recollections; he refers to them as "enduring benchmarks . . . places where we line up our own lives with the course of history itself and say 'I was there'."[12]

Social Context

Whereas aspects of the physical context dominated the recollections of several members of the family that had visited the Natural History Museum in London, social context dominated the memories of others. For the great-grandmother, grandmother, and mother, the visit apparently served primarily a social purpose. The recollections of these three are full of concerns about the well-being or enjoyment of other members of the group; matters of social management (schedules, lunch, physical comfort) kept emerging. The major recollection of the great-grandmother was of the gifts she had bought for her grandchildren still at home. It is interesting to note that 97 percent of all people we have interviewed can recall at least one person who accompanied them on the visit. Given the importance of the social context to what is learned and remembered, the role of social interaction in museum learning deserves more study.

Physical Context

All persons we interviewed could place the visit in both the temporal context and geographical contexts. "I went there when I was eight or ten years old as part of a visit to Washington," was a typical statement. Time and place appeared to be strongly linked in memory. E. Tulving has categorized this kind of memory for events as "episodic memory."[13] People consistently recall temporal aspects of their visit. H. L. Roediger and R. G. Crowder state that recollection of the temporal context of a learning situation is a crucial ingredient in successfully remembering the details of an episode.[14]

Virtually all those interviewed mentioned, without prompting, something about the physical setting. Most described the feel and gestalt of the museum. Physical size and the complexity of the layout seemed to be salient, particularly for the children. Adults showed cognizance of the functional architecture—for example, going upstairs, which exhibits were "to the right" and which were "to the left." The ability to use the functional aspect of the physical setting seems to be important in the recollection of other aspects of the experience.[15] Anyone who has lost his keys knows how important it can be to retrace his steps in looking for them, and there are types of kinesthetic learning in which both mentally and physically visualizing steps are important.[16]

Many children's recollections of field trips to zoos, farms, and nature centers include memories of smells, heat, or physical discomfort, such as mosquitoes, getting their feet wet, or getting muddy.[17] Architectural gestalt played a significant role in the recollections of fourteen museum professionals interviewed; occasionally, it played the dominant role.[18] Most people we have interviewed spontaneously described the physical setting of the museum.

Recollections of specific things seen or done, as expected, varied dramatically. Almost all those interviewed recalled at least some of the exhibits. Among the six family members who visited the British Natural History Museum, the adults seemed to have greater difficulty recalling accurately details about exhibits than did the children. The children could describe in modest detail many exhibits and, in more explicit detail, one or two exhibits. Again, recall seemed to be related to earlier interest and knowledge.

The children visiting the British Natural History Museum, in particular, seemed extremely interested in the contents of the museum; one seemed fixated on the "stuffed" nature of the specimens, perhaps reflecting disappointment at not seeing "real" animals. Both were very interested in the dinosaurs, a particular interest of theirs at the time. This was not their first exposure to fossils and preserved specimens, but it probably served to reinforce their interest in dinosaurs and their concepts of them. Their learning was very concrete as is appropriate for their ages (seven and eight at the time). Indeed, almost all recollections of childhood visits are of a concrete nature—such as the size, shape, and peculiar features of Lindbergh's plane, for example, or the hair of a wooly mammoth. The evidence of object and concept learning on the part of adults, in contrast, is less impressive. Recollections of adult visits show that social concerns often seem more important than museum content.

In our study of museum professionals' recollections of early museum experience, we found that, invariably, one or two exhibits stood out in memory.[19] This appeared to be true also in the study of early school field trip recollections.[20] One museum professional recalled, for example, an interactive exhibit at the Metropolitan Museum of Art, and standing in front of it for long periods of time pushing the same button over and over again; another museum professional recalled being scared by the plethora of large stuffed animals crowded into a dark, musty museum hall. Most first museum memories were highly personalized and often focused on a single event or detail.

In addition to recalling exhibits, several people we have interviewed recalled other activities such as eating, going to the restroom, and gift purchasing. Gift shops and gift shop purchases figured prominently in about 15 percent of the museum recollections we collected. Some people related that they still possessed museum items purchased as many as twenty or thirty years earlier.[21] Time appeared to be important for museum visitors;[22] even young children were able to recall how long they were in a museum, although we do not know how accurate their recollections are.[23] Recollections of how much time was spent in the museum were less vivid than the *perception* of time spent; visitors who did not have enough time to see all they wanted were likely to say "time flew by," and those who recalled being bored wanted to leave sooner than allowed. Such perceptions are highly personal and influence all learning in museums.

Although visitors might recall a specific object or event vividly, overall recollections of the things seen or done were vague and general. As Donald Norman states: "It is a general property of memory that we store only partial descriptions of the things to be remembered, descriptions that are sufficiently precise to work at the time something is learned, but may not [be sufficient] later on . . ."[24]

The Museum Experience as Learning

Museum visitors do not catalogue visual memories of objects and labels in academic, conceptual schemes, but assimilate events and observations in mental categories of personal significance and character, determined by events in their lives before and after the museum visit.[25] This is our definition of learning in this book. What separates learning from experience is that not all experiences are so assimilated; those that are can be said to have been learned. We would assert that the recollections reflected in our interviews are not only what people *remember* but what they *learned* from their museum experience.

If we define learning thus, we must consider the role of cuing. The people we interviewed probably saw, and perhaps remembered, much more than they revealed in the interviews. It is possible that, with appropriate cuing, they would have recalled additional exhibit memories. In both the Fivush et al. and Wolins studies, repeated cuing was used to elicit greater recall from children.[26] None of the subjects in our studies was specifically asked what he "learned" from his museum experience, nor was understanding of concepts pursued. We did ask people to recall their museum experience; thus, what we received were unbiased responses as to the events, objects, and relationships associated in people's minds with the word "museum." They may, in fact, have learned many other things, but did not associate them with their museum visit.

Creation of Meaningful, Long-Term Learning Two important mechanisms appear to be working to determine why people remember and learn certain things but not others. The first mechanism is previous knowledge.[27] For one visitor, who knew from school of Lindbergh's flight and who knew what the *Spirit of St. Louis* was, the combination of previous knowledge and the real object produced an indelible memory. The experience of seeing tangible examples of previous learning plays a major role in producing long-term learning.

Subsequent experience is the other mechanism of learning. Several researchers have hypothesized that repetition is the major mechanism for retention of memories over long periods of time.[28] Approximately 65 percent of persons asked if they had ever thought about an early childhood field trip experience later in their life reported that they had.[29]

We think it is likely that previous experience and subsequent reinforcement are equally important components of long-term learning. Previous knowledge presupposes that memories were laid down, and reinforcement ensures that memories are retained. Our interviews show how memories are bound together in ways that may make sense to the individual but not necessarily to another person. Memories are not like photographs of events, but rather like pieces of information collected from many events. Research by E. F. Loftus and J. C. Palmer, support this idea. They state: "Two kinds of information go into one's memory for some complex occurrence. The first is information gleaned during the perception of the original event; the second is external information supplied after the fact. Over time, information from these two sources may be integrated in such a way that we are unable to tell from which source some specific detail is recalled. All we have is one 'memory.'"[30]

If this proposition is true, it will be difficult both to predict what a person will learn during a museum visit and to measure that learning later because of the complex and idiosyncratic role of past and future experiences. Moreover, the three components of the Interactive Experience Model, all of which are involved in the visitor's museum learning, are not easily distinguishable or separable.

To the extent that learning appears to require both previous experience and subsequent reinforcement, it follows that people with greater previous experience are likely to learn more than people with less experience. Moreover, learning and memory rarely reflect pure encoding of experiences, but rather are composites of experiences constructed from a person's store of knowledge and understanding.

We would argue that museum learning is a complex interactive experience, incorporating diverse contexts, as well as a profoundly durable kind of learning. We would also conclude that diverse kinds of long-term, meaningful learning take place in museums: social learning, spatial learning, concept learning, and aesthetic learning. These insights into museum learning have profound implications for museum practice. Museums have not always structured their settings to offer the kinds of experiences either the visitor or the museum most desires. A better understanding of how and what visitors learn should make it possible to improve the quality of museum visits.

SECTION IV

A Professional's Guide to the Museum Experience

9.
Creating the Museum Experience

Museum staff invest a great deal of time in designing exhibitions and programs that will communicate important ideas to the public; yet the evidence shows that not all messages get across to visitors, and that visitors do not always come away from the museum having reaped the expected benefits. Museums may be pleased to hear that visitors find them socially and aesthetically enriching environments, but is that enough? A museum is supposed to provide intellectually important ideas to the public—the very ideas that so few of the public seem to recall or associate directly with their museum experience.

We should not ignore, however, the positive aspects of research findings, in particular, the remarkable durability of museum recollections. Obviously, museum experiences can be deeply imbedded in visitors' memories, with potential for significant learning.

How can we ensure that more of visitors' durable memories are ideas the museum wishes to convey? We need to work harder at two levels. First, we must reshape institutional goals to make them more compatible with what we currently know about visitors' experiences. This means acknowledging the importance of goals visitors have other than those related to facts and concepts. Second, we must enhance museum experiences so they will yield meaningful learning more in line with these goals. How do we create powerful museum experiences that result in multiple kinds of learning, including concept-related learning?

The Interactive Experience Model, with its emphasis on the interaction among personal, social, and physical contexts, could be a useful aid for institutions in setting goals and recrafting museum education efforts. The model is useful not only for conceptualizing the museum experience, but also for creating effective museum experiences for visitors. Applying the Interactive Experience Model to practice requires rethinking the role museums play in visitors' lives as well as realigning the focus of museum education efforts. The key is to create an environment in which the visitor becomes part of a seamless array of mutually reinforcing contexts which separately and collectively support the museum's goals. In such a scheme, the museum professional would create not only exhibits and programs, but also museum experiences. In this chapter we address use of the model to shape institutional goals and, in the following two chapters, the implications of the model for casual visitors and organized groups.

Institutional Goals for Enhancing the Visitor's Experience

How do we develop institutional goals that translate into an array of mutually reinforcing contexts? To begin, we must try to visualize the entire museum experience, build on the visitor's past experience, and support the visitor's future experiences. We need to understand how the visitor's one- or two-hour experience in the museum will fit into her life. How do visitors use the information they encounter in the museum? Do they think they might someday want to use this information? Do exhibitions, programs, brochures, gift shops, restrooms, parking lots, guards, and maps all work together to create a series of mutually reinforcing contexts for the visitor? The entire institution must unite to make the visitor's experience resemble the experience the museum wishes the visitor to have.

Many museums would claim to have done this; few museums are without mission statements and explicitly stated institutional goals. But very few museums scrutinize each activity to determine how it contributes to the total package of visitor experiences. How many museums can assert that they have tried to ensure that every visitor leaves the institution with an understanding of what the museum wished to communicate?

Conceptualizing institutional goals is one thing; reconciling them with the realities of visitor interests and behavior is another. Museums must appreciate the limitations within which they work. The vast majority of museum visitors come through institutions fleetingly; with luck, they will visit two or more times in their lives, but many will visit only once. A few hours of a person's life is not much.

What can a museum do in a few hours that will have an effect on a visitor? This question must constantly be asked, and realistic expectations established. Perhaps the visitor cannot become an expert on Victorian furnishings or Jurassic biology in one hour, but we stand a chance of imparting in an hour the idea that Victorian furniture is different from Georgian furniture, that natural ecosystems are important to our well-being, and that modern art can be appreciated.

There is no guarantee that merely adopting a few well-selected goals is the solution; any change in the visitor will be difficult, given the constraints under which museums operate. It is important to understand those constraints so that we can work with them instead of against them. Without limiting what is displayed or how visitors interact with displays, it is essential that visitors know that the museum holds dear a few well-selected goals. Visitors want to know what the museum values, yet often visitors leave museums without a clue. One reason that few visitors' museum recollections are of objects or concepts is that museum presentations are often unfocused and ambiguous in their priorities. Visitors experience the museum as a smorgasbord of unrelated objects, images, and ideas, few of which strike a sufficiently resonating chord to be recalled years later. We need strategies for presentation that will ensure clear and unambiguous concept learning.

Having stated the importance of concept-oriented goals,

we must emphasize that the museum experience is more than the learning of concepts. Museums function admirably as facilitators of social, aesthetic, and often kinesthetic learning, and should define these goals clearly along with their conceptual goals. Making these goals explicit will go a long way toward improving the quality of the visitor's experience.

Nested Goals Identification of institutional goals requires long-range planning. The planning we propose is the development of a series of nested goals—like Russian dolls within dolls within dolls. The process involves defining a series of progressively more specific perspectives on what each component of the museum is attempting to accomplish within the realm of the visitor experience.

The place to begin is with the museum's public image. How should the public view the institution? If it could play word association games with the public, what words would the museum like the public to associate with it? What are the public relations goals for the museum?

Next should be the issue of audience. What audiences should the museum be attracting? What messages does the museum wish to convey to these audiences? Should the message be the same for all audiences, or different for certain groups? Should some audiences be more important than others? Should some audiences be deemed of higher priority than others? What are the institutional goals relative to underserved audiences, and how do these fit into overall institutional priorities?

Once these goals have been defined, the museum can begin to think about the features of the building. What should the goal be for museum access—parking lots, stairs, access for the disabled, entry ways, outside signs? What should the goals be for exhibitions as a whole? What should the goals of the gift shop and restaurant be? What should the goal of the entrance area be? The restrooms? The orientation devices?

What should the goals be for the staff who interact directly with the public—the guards, ticket sellers, information people, and on-the-floor explainers? What message should these individuals communicate? Should telephones be answered by people or by answering machines? More is at stake than finances; all interactions with the public convey messages.

What are the goals for each and every exhibit, hand-out, catalogue, brochure, public program, and press release? How do these contribute to the larger goals? The details of everyday operation and practice—every facet of the museum's interface with the public—can be analyzed. The process, if successful, will not only help to clarify and define the operational side of the institution but will inevitably affect acquisitions, fund raising, and personnel decisions as well. What we propose here is a blueprint for a visitor-centered view of museum management, a view that appreciates the ever-growing importance of public activities in the life and well-being of the museum.

The Interactive Experience Model as Overlay

The central premise of this book has been that the visitor's museum experience is directly affected by the interaction of the personal, social, and physical contexts. No matter how well-conceived a goal may be in concept, unless it can be articulated in a contextually appropriate manner it will not succeed. The approach we propose, after going through the nested goals process described above, is to think of each of the three contexts as "overlays" that affect, or color, each goal. In the following two chapters, we present specific recommendations that should help this process.

10.
Creating Museum Experiences for Casual Visitors

Most museum visitors are casual visitors, not pre-arranged, institutionally organized groups. Exhibitions are the major media through which museums communicate with the public. Through object placement and display, graphic and video presentation, and label content, museums hope to influence the thoughts, feelings, and, ultimately, the learning of the casual visiting public. To be effective, as we have noted, exhibitions should be designed to reinforce both the experiences the visitor has inside the museum and those outside, before and after the visit. How can we design museum exhibitions to be more visitor-centered?

In designing an exhibit, setting goals is critical. The process should begin with the conceptualization of the exhibit and be revisited throughout planning and development. There should be concept-oriented goals, but also affective and psychomotor goals for the learning aspects of the museum experience. If an exhibition has a number of different components, nested goals can be used to build complexity and layers into the process. If an exhibit has five parts, for example, one would expect five nested sub-goals, each contributing to the overall goal of the exhibit. The final step in exhibition goal-setting should be to apply the three contexts of the Interactive Experience Model to analyze the "contextual overlays" that might influence the visitor's interaction with the exhibit. Nine general principles follow from the

Interactive Experience Model that may be useful as a framework for setting exhibit goals.

Personal Context

1. **Each visitor learns in a different way, and interprets information through the lens of previous knowledge, experience, and beliefs.**

   This principle represents a significant challenge to museums in general, and to exhibition designers and developers in particular. It suggests that exhibit content needs to be presented with multiple entry and exit points. Moreover, information should be presented in different ways. The best way to ensure that exhibit content and presentation are responsive to visitors' personal contexts is to conduct front-end evaluation. With the goals of the exhibit clearly in mind, move to the floor of the museum and talk to visitors. Do the visitors already know these concepts? Are they familiar with the vocabulary, but unsure of the definitions? What are their attitudes on the subject?

   When the National Museum of Natural History recently redesigned its Marine Life Hall, it wanted to show the complexity and interdependence of marine ecosystems and the role people could play in preserving these systems. A front-end evaluation revealed that the public not only did not know what an ecosystem was, but was not even familiar with the word; in contrast, the public had a reasonable understanding of the word "system." This suggested that using the word "ecosystem" in the title and initial orientation film as originally planned would merely confuse the public, and the exhibition would be better off starting with a word like "system" with which the public already had some familiarity.[1] The same front-end evaluation revealed that the public overwhelmingly believed that marine systems should be preserved, but they had no clue as to why, or how this could be accomplished. Consequently, the exhibition team realized it did not need to convince the public to preserve marine environments, but should focus on why that was important and how each person could help the effort.[2]

Another important question to resolve during front-end evaluation is whether or not the public has any expectations of what an exhibit will be about or how it will be presented. Visitors generally do not have strong expectations about exhibits or presentation, but when they do, they are worth noting. We cited the case of a museum that inserted a hands-on exhibit in the middle of a hands-off institution, an example of violating visitors' expectations. Through front-end evaluation, it should have been possible to predict and avoid this problem.

Again, professionals involved in exhibition development should look beyond the exhibit to the visitor's experience. It is appropriate, given the nature of museums, that exhibits be driven by content, as defined by a curator or other subject matter specialist, but when content becomes the only consideration it reduces the effectiveness of exhibits. A better approach is to find ways to use the content to create visitor experiences, or to find ways to create visitor experiences that involve the content. The museum should also consider experiences it would like the visitor to have while interacting with the exhibit, and ask how the content can be woven into this experience. One approach is through multi-sensory and multi-media techniques, which help audiences acquire information through visual, aural, and tactile means. These technologies can assist in creating experiences for visitors which highly contextualize the objects.*

Exhibit creators need to understand what the visitor already knows as well as what the museum wants the visitor ultimately to know. The task of the exhibition team is to bridge these two points, to build structures that enable visitors to traverse the path from current knowledge and experience to hoped-for knowledge and experience. This is a difficult task under any circumstances, but an impossible task if the two end points are not well known and appreciated.

---

*Technology, of course, is no panacea, and is effective only when its use is well thought out and the integrity of the content of an exhibit is retained.

Assuming that the exhibition planning team has done its front-end evaluation and identified visitors' knowledge, attitudes, and expectations, how does it use this information to design exhibits that will accommodate a broad range of visitors? The most common approach has been to design exhibits with multiple layers—parts for the neophyte and parts for the expert, parts for the visitor spending five minutes and parts for the visitor spending fifty minutes. Another approach is to design some exhibits specifically for first-time visitors and some specifically for frequent, or expert, visitors. Virtually every other type of educational institution offers tiered instruction; museums can also. Some museums have tried this on a small, experimental scale with special exhibitions, but more museums could try permanent exhibits geared to particular knowledge levels, ages, or cultural backgrounds.

Different people value different leisure-time activities, and it may not be possible to accommodate everyone's agenda with a single approach or within a single exhibit. To design exhibits to fill the needs of those who do visit the museum, rather than those the museum would like to attract, is not to exclude new audiences but to recognize that serving even current audiences adequately is a challenge in itself.

2. All visitors personalize the museum's message to conform to their own understanding and experience.

Even though many museum professionals consider their objects to be only as valuable as the ideas they convey, it remains the objects that distinguish museums from other institutions. In general, the public finds "things" fascinating and easy to understand. Given the limited time visitors are in exhibition spaces, museum staff need to distinguish between ideas that can and cannot be communicated through exhibitions.

Remember the importance of context. Placing an object within an appropriate and comprehensible context will significantly enhance the visitor's ability to comprehend an object's use and value. If a museum can design an exhibit that allows the visitor to walk away remembering what a thing looked like, how it was used, and how it relates to the visitor, the museum has designed a very good exhibit.

Visitors tend to compare an object on display to an object they have seen before. A visitor will say, "Doesn't that painting remind you of the coast of Maine?" or "My grandmother used to have a shawl just like that one." Although frustrating for museum professionals, visitors will always try to understand an exhibit in the context of their own experiences. Museum professionals do not always present objects with this in mind because often they have already personalized their *own* knowledge and level of understanding of the objects.

Successful exhibits facilitate the visitor's ability to personalize objects and ideas; unsuccessful exhibits create barriers to visitor personalization. Visitors should be encouraged to personalize the exhibit. This can be done through labels, humor, theater, live interpreters, contextual arrangement of objects, or videos that begin with the familiar and move to the unfamiliar.

Abstract ideas are built upon a solid foundation of concrete understanding. Museums that wish to convey an abstract message should be sure to ground it in the concrete—and the concrete of a novice, not that of an expert. This grounding needs to begin at conceptualization of the exhibit, not just when label copy is being written. Deciding on a few major messages and providing "cognitive hooks" that will relate the material to that of a lay person is critical and needs to be a part of the exhibition process from the very beginning.

The Natural History Museum in London did an excellent job of providing a concrete introduction to an otherwise abstract idea in its Hall of Human Evolution. To understand human evolution, the visitor needs first to have some understanding of life in general, and vertebrate, mammalian, and primate evolution in particular. How does one provide a useful overview of these relationships without the overview becoming the exhibit? At the entrance of the exhibition, the museum installed a large case full of different animals, including insects, crabs, gorillas, birds, snakes, monkeys, lions, fish, and people. The label said: "These are all animals." The next case took all the same organisms and separated them in two cases, animals without backbones and animals with backbones; each had an appropriate, short label. Then they divided all the vertebrates in the case into two cases, mammals and non-mammals; then they divided all mammals in the case again, separating primates and non-primates. Finally, they had a case of anthropoid apes, including gorillas, chimps, humans, and gibbons, and another case with the remaining monkeys. Thus, in a series of cases with a minimum of labels they were able to provide directly, concretely, and elegantly a sense of the morphological differences between anthropoid apes and all other forms of animal life.

Once the preliminary design and message have been decided, museums should create prototypes and test assumptions through formative evaluation. Much as in front-end evaluation, the key to high-quality formative evaluation is a continuing dialogue with visitors. Interviewing visitors is an obvious way to conduct formative evaluation, but there are other techniques worth considering. One which has been used for years in marketing is the focus group, a small group of people who either share an experience and then collectively discuss their reactions to it, or can be asked to discuss alternative actions. For example, a museum could invite small groups of visitors to an exhibition development area or show them a preliminary video, then lead them in a discussion of their reactions. A major advantage of focus groups is that people in a small group will often share feelings and opinions they would be unwilling to share in a face-to-face interview. The group atmosphere can also produce a brainstorming session that yields creative or unorthodox suggestions of significant value.[3]

Another effective formative evaluation tool is the structured observation, both watching and listening to visitors. For example, museums can listen to conversations of visitors while they view preliminary films or mock-ups. How do they personalize the experience? Are they forced to create their own cognitive framework, or has the exhibit already provided an easily accessible one? Do visitors read labels and, if they do, which ones? Do visitors' conversations reflect the intent of the exhibit or not?

3. Every visitor arrives with an agenda and a set of expectations for what the museum visit will hold.

Visitor agendas and expectations are not always what a museum would like them to be. As Samuel Taylor, Director of Exhibitions at the American Museum of Natural History, recently quipped, "Most people don't wake up on Saturday morning and say, 'Let's go to the aquarium today and learn about teleost adaptations.'"[4] There may be many reasons why visitors go to museums, including educational reasons, but few visitors set out to learn the specific information contained in a particular exhibition. Visitors' interests are much more general, and a large part of their general agenda is to have fun.

The words "fun," "enjoyment," and "entertainment" are used a great deal in the museum world these days. Invariably, the comparison comes around to Disneyland. The idea that museums should become more like theme parks has split the museum world between those horrified by the prospect and those who embrace the notion. Neither extreme is useful; museums need not try to compete with Disneyland, but they should accept that they are competing for visitor's leisure time and they need to be attuned to the needs and desires of their consumers. Disneyland knows its customers, what its product is, and how to deliver it.

Museums have not always been as attuned to their clientele. Although evidence suggests that occasional visitors *do* make choices between amusement parks and museums, and vice versa, the research on leisure suggests that the public generally recognizes that they serve different purposes and fulfill different leisure needs. Current trends suggest that the traditional distinctions between theme parks and museums may be blurring, however. For example, Epcot Center in Disney World in Orlando, Florida, increasingly uses educational and cultural exhibitions.

Visitors to museums want to have the fun of seeing strange and unusual things, of being visually stimulated and intellectually challenged. This used to be the unique domain of the museum. As theme parks expand their offerings, museum staff will have to work harder to define their niche in the leisure market.

The object is to reconcile the museum's agenda for the visitor with the visitor's own agenda. These agendas need not be mutually exclusive, though historically they often have been. Museums, for example, do not try to prevent visitors from having an enjoyable visit, nor does the visitor object to an educational message; in fact, the visitor expects it and would be disappointed if there were no educational value to a museum experience. But the visitor also wishes to have a pleasant time with his social group.

To make exhibits facilitate learning, museum professionals should begin the exhibit design process by thinking about how the visitor might use the knowledge presented in the exhibits rather than thinking about what objects to exhibit or what ideas to present. This perspective will significantly increase the probability for overlap between the visitor's and the museum's agendas.

Making museums entertaining does not mean trivializing exhibits, but it does suggest designing exhibition spaces that encourage a variety of emotional responses.[5] Entertaining exhibits actively engage the visitor intellectually and physically. Successful museum exhibits have labels that pose questions, or interpreters who pose questions to the visitor and demonstrate principles or phenomena that focus the visitor's attention. Exhibits should invite visitors to participate and become intellectually involved, let visitors touch objects, manipulate machines, smell an environment, and hear sounds. Here, properly applied, multi-media techniques can be useful. The combination of intellectual and physical involvement is the essence of an interactive exhibit and an interactive museum. The interaction between museum and visitor should not be limited to exhibits but should extend to the gift shop, food service, and all areas of the museum.

Social Context

4. Most visitors come to the museum as part of a social group, and what visitors see, do, and remember is mediated by that group.

Museums are social settings, yet many museums create significant barriers to social exchange. Some museums discourage conversation by encouraging silence (the library model of behavior setting); other museums are so noisy that conversation is impossible. The level and organization of the content often impede conversation as well; if information is highly technical or dry, it can be difficult for families to converse about it. How easy does the museum make it to have a conversation about the objects being viewed?

The physical setting can impede social interactions as well; often exhibits are built so only one person at a time can use them. For example, interactive computer exhibits are notorious for limiting multiple access. Exhibits that create lines of visitors moving single file in front of them also discourage social interaction. What are some alternatives?

Because families make up a significant percentage of visitors to museums, displays should be designed to be seen from both adult and child heights; displays and labels should be comprehensible to both children and adults; and exhibits intended for family groups should permit group participation. The Maryland Science Center in Baltimore provides a nice example. The first thing that used to greet visitors to the museum was an array of machine-driven interactive science exhibits. The gestalt was flashing lights, loud noises, and darting children—exciting but not very conducive to social interaction. Recently, the museum moved these "science arcade" exhibits up to the third floor, carpeted the first floor to dampen the noise, and installed low-tech, manipulative exhibits and games that encourage group participation. Family groups can now be seen sorting feathers, doing puzzles together, and actively conversing. Rather than create immediate obstacles to family group use, the museum set a tone for the visit by creating an initial experience that promoted family social interactions.

But social groups are diverse, and what works for one kind may not necessarily work for all. For example, one museum designed an exhibit that required twenty people to work cooperatively to solve a problem. The exhibit worked wonderfully during the week when school groups of twenty children from the same class would work together, but it had serious problems on weekends, when visitors in small groups were reluctant to cooperate with perfect strangers to solve the problem. It is difficult to make a single exhibit work for all people at all times.

Museums could create some exhibits specifically for all-adult groups, some for individuals, some for school groups, and some for family groups of varying ages, keeping in mind that some families will be independent-learning families and will prefer to have a more solitary experience, while some share experiences with other people, even strangers. As museums make their exhibits more accessible to diverse audiences, they should remember that some extended family groups come in larger numbers and cannot interact in spaces designed for only a few people.

The sharing of information within the social group is both a benefit and a bane of social interaction. Parents share stories and "explain" the exhibits to children. Adults impress each other with their knowledge of the subject matter. When these exchanges go well, the quantity of information transfer is tremendous; when they go wrong, information is still transferred, but not always the information desired by the exhibit team.

There is no such thing as a "visitor-proof" exhibit, nor should museum staff seek such a goal; exhibits should encourage inter-group communication. The key to maximizing good communication resides once again in providing comprehensible and visitor-centered exhibits. If a parent is asked by a child to explain an exhibit and does not know what that exhibit is about, the chances are the parent will fake it. Museums can help these parents by finding out through evaluation procedures what kinds of questions are likely to arise and then providing the answers.

Visitors personalize each exhibit, frequently as a vehicle

for facilitating social bonding. These bonds, too, can be anticipated by front-end and formative evaluation and incorporated directly in the design of the exhibit.

5. The visitor's experience within the museum includes docents, guards, concessionaires, and other visitors.

We would strongly endorse integrating people in the exhibit design whenever possible. Some of the most striking museum exhibits have been those in which people played an integral role in the exhibit as live artisans, musicians, scientists, and interpreters. When real people are integrated in an exhibit, visitors can appreciate the scale of an object and its relationship to the world beyond the museum. This is the essence of living history sites and nature centers, and the goal of modern zoos, aquaria, and arboreta—to provide meaningful and realistic settings in which to understand history, biology, and other subjects.

A major problem at many museums is crowding, and crowds are not always easy to control. Most people have only limited tolerance for crowded places. We have all seen exhibits that seem wonderful in an empty exhibit hall, but that under more normal conditions with many people around become unusable. Exhibits need to be designed and evaluated with not only the ultimate users in mind, but also the normal configuration of those users.

Museum staff are occasionally dismayed that guards, who have no training or mandate, interpret exhibits for visitors. Michael Spock at the Field Museum of Natural History recognized that while many daytime guards were charged with security functions, others at cash registers, in the coat check room, and supervising school groups were providing direct service to visitors. These guards now have been given training in multi-cultural communication and interpretation, have participated in the review of labels for new exhibits, and are generally encouraged to view themselves as responsible for visitor comfort and enjoyment.

Museum staff and docents have played a longstanding role in helping to interpret exhibits to the public, but historically they have been left completely out of exhibit development. Recently, many museums have attempted to bring educational staff and volunteers into the exhibition development process early, letting them suggest how exhibits should be designed to facilitate interpretation. This is a positive approach to exhibition design; ultimately, the human link between the exhibit and the visitor is likely to be the most important determinant of public understanding and learning. It is important that educators participating in the exhibition process be knowledgeable about the public, however. This is not necessarily a given, and not all educators are suited to or qualified for the job.

Physical Context

6. Visitors are drawn to museums because they contain objects outside their normal experience. Visitors come to "look" in a variety of ways.

Visitors come to museums to see unique objects. Any museum would be well advised to do some basic market research to determine what the community perceives to be unique about it. It is essential to know what the public thinks is unique in the setting in order to design exhibits that reinforce or modify these perceptions.

If the community thinks that a museum contains only priceless art, what does it think of an exhibition of minimalist "junk" sculptures? Can the museum communicate the artistic role of this work in post-modern American art? If the public thinks a museum is a place to see "neat scientific stuff," what does this suggest for an exhibition on common household chemicals? The question is how best to enhance the public's experience within a museum. Given the public's often lofty expectations for institutions, it is important to acknowledge these feelings and satisfy those expectations. This means that we need to take extra steps when exhibitions do not obviously meet the expectations of our visitors.

Graburn talked about the visitor's sense of reverence toward the museum,[6] not just in the larger sense of awe, but in esteem for the importance of its collection, for the museum provides legitimacy for the objects contained within.

This is a point made explicitly by Anthony Shelton (cited in Weil, 1991) in relation to the aesthetic value of a piece of art, but it clearly applies to all museum objects.[7] According to Shelton, the value of an object is not a function of the creator of the object but a function of the museum or other validating institution that consecrates or in some other way legitimizes the work. The public has no problems when the legitimacy is obvious and historical; the public has considerable difficulty when the legitimacy is not apparent or recent in origin. The exhibit development team must be sensitive to this issue lest these "value" discrepancies discredit the exhibit.

7. **Visitors are strongly influenced by the physical aspects of museums, including the architecture, ambience, smell, sounds, and the "feel" of the place.**

Perhaps the most difficult task facing a museum exhibit developer or educator is to assess accurately the visitor's level of experience and information. Being able to put oneself in the visitor's shoes is truly a gift. This task is particularly important in the area of the physical setting. Many of us can be naïve about subject matter. Exhibit professionals, rightly or wrongly, are always claiming to know as little as the public about the subject matter, but everyone in the museum is an expert compared to the public when it comes to the physical setting. Once one has entered a new physical setting, it is no longer new; but many of the museum's visitors are there for the first time. What is it like to be a first-time visitor?

The first time one is in a new environment loaded with sensory novelty, one experiences that setting through all the senses. The research on long-term recollections demonstrates this sensory, rather than cognitive, experiencing of museums, particularly for first-time visitors. It is imperative when designing an exhibit to try to understand how visitors will experience it. Feeling disoriented, finding no places to sit down and relax, or not being sure of the location of the nearest restroom can all contribute to an unhappy experience. Maslow's hierarchy of needs is useful in designing an exhibition; a museum that attends to visitors' physical needs will be able to address their intellects.

In an excellent article on zoos, Lars Anderson stated that "An ugly fence, for example, may be distracting; so may a dirty pathway or an unpleasant smell. If negative experiences dominate, all efforts at interpretation will be in vain no matter how skillfully conceived and implemented. Visitors will leave the exhibit remembering only the negative experience, not the information that was imparted."[8] In the same article, Anderson cited Linda Taylor's observation that if visitors read the words "extremely rare" on a beat-up plank of wood alongside a certain animal enclosure, many will wonder why, if these things are so precious, somebody doesn't paint a new sign and clean the fence?[9]

In exhibit design, settings should reinforce the context the museum wishes to communicate. William Conway said it eloquently in his classic article, "How to Exhibit a Bullfrog."[10] "When a visitor gets off the bus and enters your gate, he should be in a world of wild creatures. In so far as possible, your buildings should be concealed. Zoo construction should not simply provide some architect a chance to erect a masonry memorial to himself. If you must erect buildings, don't . . . crowd them into some formal agglomeration that looks like a shopping center. Surround your zoo-goers with plants and animals." There is some evidence that creating such spaces can facilitate visitor learning. In a study at Zoo Atlanta, researchers found that attitudes toward animals were far more positive when the animals were displayed in a natural habitat than in a traditional cage.[11] Current efforts to create what are called "immersion exhibitions" reflect this growing awareness.[12] The museum space—all its exhibits, shops, and amenities—should embody the context it wishes to create.

8. Visitors encounter an array of experiences from which they select a small number.

This principle is about humility. One can design the most wonderful exhibit, but if no one looks at it, it is not wonderful. Slick graphics, expensive computer hardware and software, and priceless objects do not guarantee visitor attention; exhibits that "speak to" the visitor, that stimulate curiosity and provide a greater understanding of how the visitor fits into the world, are successful.

Years of "attracting power" and "holding power" research have resulted in rows of exhibits embellished with a multitude of bells and whistles, but the key to engaging the visitor turns out to be at once simpler and more complicated. Visitors may become physically engaged with exhibits featuring bells and whistles, but there is little evidence to support intellectual engagement in the absence of something that piques a visitor's curiosity or directly relates to the visitor's own interests. Intellectually engaging exhibits do not have to be fancy or expensive. Although it is not always possible to predict what will engage visitors intellectually, it is possible with front-end and formative evaluation to determine what does not engage visitors. The driving force in the design of exhibits has to be the visitor's response.

9. The visitor's attention is strongly influenced by the location of exhibits and by the museum's orientation.

Even with orientation, the museum staff must accept the fact that those exhibits closest to the front door will get the most exposure. Attempts to get visitors to the back of the museum by putting popular exhibits there have been only marginally successful. Exhibits intended for infrequent visitors should be by the front door; those for regular visitors can be upstairs and in back because the regular visitors will know or find out how to get there. The same principles should apply to the placement of information within an exhibition—the most important stuff should be up front.

Orientation within the museum, orientation within an exhibit, and general placement of an exhibit relative to other exhibits in the museum can dramatically affect visitor response and behavior. It is impossible, as has been attempted in the past, to consider one particular exhibit component in isolation from the whole. One can no more predict how a particular exhibit element will function in isolation from the entire exhibition than one can understand how a particular exhibition will function in isolation from the entire museum experience. This fact has profound implications for the issue of museum evaluation.

Despite the best laid plans of even the most conscientious exhibit planners, visitors will not always use the exhibit in the way it is intended; some visitors seem to go out of their way to foil the exhibit planner. Therefore, museums should avoid, when possible, organizing exhibits sequentially, because some visitors will view the exhibit out of sequence. If the best way to organize an exhibition is sequentially, then it is important to inform the visitor that the sequence is important. Subtle messages will not suffice.

Finally, not all visitors are equally able to use the museum for educational purposes. Disabled visitors may not be able to gain access to all of the information provided, and many senior citizens have impaired sight and hearing which prevent them from using some exhibit elements. Special labels, large graphics, or supplementary audio information may provide the extra assistance these visitors require. A number of museums have made the surprising discovery that materials developed for such visitors have been preferred by other visitors as well!

Sometimes, just the differences in the chunking ability of experienced and inexperienced visitors can cause problems. Once again, special labels and other interpretive devices such as audios, graphics, computer interactives, or hands-on experiences that assist the unsavvy visitor by providing him with prompts or helping him focus attention on relevant attributes may be worth pursuing. The skill of knowing "what to look for" or "how to do" the museum makes it easier for visitors to relate what they see to their own experience. Museum savvy provides the visitor a level of control over the museum experience that makes the visit more intrinsically satisfying. Every visitor deserves to feel comfortable in experiencing the museum.

11.
Creating Museum Experiences for Organized Groups

O rganized programs for specific audiences represent a major element of a museum's contribution to public learning. School field trips, public programs, and educational outreach programs remain a major activity of museum education departments, while new programs for other sectors of the public, such as senior citizens, family groups, or foreign visitors, continue to grow.

Like casual visitors, groups are influenced by a host of factors within the museum setting, but most significantly by the educational program designed for them. Programs are designed to be age-appropriate, accurate in content, and enjoyable. They are also designed to provide high-quality concept learning opportunities, particularly for school groups.

Organized groups, like casual visitors, tend to leave the museum without taking with them many of the messages intended. This can be particularly disheartening because there is often a higher human investment in programs for groups. Again, the complexity of the visitors' museum experience is often not taken sufficiently into account when programs are planned and implemented. To be effective, programs should be designed to be contextually reinforcing experiences for the group, supporting both the experiences within the museum and those outside the museum before and after the visit. How does one design educational programs that are more visitor-centered and that have the greatest influence on the visitor?

Again, goal-setting should begin with early conceptualization of the program and be revisited throughout the planning and implementation of the program. Both concept-oriented goals and goals focusing on the affective and psychomotor aspects of the museum experience should be defined. If different components contribute to the program, goals can be grouped to build complexity and layers into them. The final step should be to apply the Interactive Experience Model as contextual overlays that might influence the visitor's interaction with the program.

Eight general principles make up the organizing framework for the program planning process. The points presented apply equally to all groups, with slight variations.

Personal Context

1. The visitor's pre-visit agenda will strongly influence in-museum behavior and learning.

The agenda may be informed by previous visits to the museum or by things that a teacher, family members, or friends have said. Occasionally, but not frequently enough, the agenda is informed by relevant information provided by the museum. Museums should, if possible, provide pre-trip information for organized groups; research on school field trips to museums has demonstrated that providing pre-trip orientation about the material to be covered consistently yields improved learning about the content presented on the field trip.[1] Children, in particular, should be informed before, during, and after a trip about the museum's and school's goals and objectives for the trip. They should understand clearly and concisely what the educator and museum expect them to do and learn while on the field trip.

Pre-trip orientation materials should not necessarily be restricted to the content to be covered. Visitors will benefit from being told what they will see, do, be able to purchase, and, if appropriate, about unusual sights and smells. The museum may have an agenda for an organized visit, but so too do the visitors. The two may not bear much resemblance; for example, research on children's groups suggests that providing relevant information before the visit pays significant dividends in concept learning.[2]

An additional purpose of pre-trip orientation is to create an optimum level of novelty, at which maximum learning occurs.[3] Striking a balance for the learner between the novelty of an unfamiliar setting and the excitement accompanying any new experience is important. Pre-trip orientation materials have proven useful for this purpose, but need not include everything that will happen. Recollection research on children who were field trip veterans (upwards of fifteen field trips per year) suggests that some deviation from "the normal script" resulted in greater likelihood of recall.[4] A few moderate surprises are useful, surprises that extend naturally from the visitor's agenda. For example, one might tell visitors that they will be seeing moon rocks during their visit to the museum, but not that they will actually be able to touch or hold one. These surprises should enhance both interest and conceptual learning.

2. **Visitors have different learning styles, and their previous experiences affect their learning from lessons in the museum.**

Gardner suggested at least seven important "intelligences."[5] Museums offer the opportunity to emphasize these. School programs, in particular, should be structured to include as many approaches as possible, not just reading labels and listening to interpreters talk. McCarthy's 4MAT learning cycle is another approach to ensuring that different ways of "knowing" and "doing" the museum are included.[6] The significance of different learning modalities is reflected in a common anecdote about school field trips in which the classroom "bad" child becomes the museum "good" child. The change in modality of museum learning frequently permits "problem" children to shine.[7]

Any good lesson must build upon previous experiences to be successful; museum trips are no exception.[8] Encouraging schools to plan field trips that build upon lessons presented during the normal curriculum is common practice. For years, schools have depended on museums to design programs that fit into existing school curricula, and most museums have willingly complied—but museums should require that schools hold up their end of the bargain. Schools should be asked how they will use a field trip to extend classroom lessons. This would help create true school/museum partnerships that would result in greater long-term benefits for the child.

A few school systems are moving toward the "integrated curriculum" approach, that is, teaching math, science, art, language, and reading skills not as separate subjects, but in an integrated way (E. Klein & J. O'Flahaven, personal communication, 1991). Museums need to be a part of this approach. School systems or individual schools that have been long-time users of the museum should be contacted at the beginning of the school year and asked what their integrated curriculum for the year is and how they plan to use the museum in that curriculum. Once again, recollection data suggest that those field trip experiences that were closely tied to school curricula were much more likely to be recalled than were field trip experiences unrelated to other school efforts.[9]

Enhanced learning depends on reinforcement of existing knowledge. The museum should seek connections between the museum experience and the visitor's life outside the museum. The more connections between what happens in the museum and what happens to people in their everyday lives, the higher the probability that the information presented will be remembered and used later in the visitor's life.

3. Visitors make sense of what they experience in the museum in a concrete way.

Every person who enters the museum as part of an organized trip will conceptualize concretely the information presented in the museum in a form that can be seen, touched, smelled, tasted, or heard. Ideas that cannot be presented concretely should not be presented at all. No matter

how adept one is at absorbing abstractions, nothing rein-
forces experience like involvement of the senses.

Although all people probably learn best when new material is presented concretely, different approaches are necessary for different ages. For example, pre-school and kindergarten children have limited fine and gross motor skills, so
activities designed for them must not depend on these skills.
Young children deal with information, particularly words,
very literally; thus, metaphors are not good devices for explaining things to pre-school and kindergarten children. In
addition, this age group can only deal with one variable at a
time, so one would not want to ask them to select, from a
group of historical hats in a case, which ones were the biggest and fuzziest, because they would focus on either the
biggest or the fuzziest, but not both at the same time. This
principle applies to directions, too. Directions should be simple and include only one step at a time.

Early elementary school-aged children can begin to deal
with multiple variables, particularly a continuum. For example, one can ask a second grader to try to determine which
of a group of birds has the longest beak and which has the
shortest. Does the bird with the longest beak also have the
longest legs? One can also give a string of two or three com-
mands and expect children of this age to follow directions.
At this age, children still think in very concrete terms. Their
fine and gross motor skills are developing, and they can be
expected to do simple drawings, puzzles, and group action
games.

By the latter half of elementary school, children should
be able to deal with multiple variables, often in their heads,
as long as the variables are still grounded in concrete reality.
One could show children in this age group a hummingbird,
let them see how long its beak is, then ask them to go out
and locate flowers that the beak would fit into. A fourth
grader should be able to keep the mental image of a hummingbird's beak in his head while walking around a botanical garden; a first grader would need a toothpick or some
other physical representation in hand while looking at flowers. The child in upper elementary school has relatively well-

developed fine and gross motor skills and the ability to express his or her thoughts and ideas orally and, to a limited extent, on paper.

By the age of twelve or thirteen, many children are adult-like, physically and intellectually, though not emotionally. Although adolescents are capable of abstract thought, there is no substitute, at any age, for tangible learning. It is also at this age that children become very social, and programs for adolescents should build on their desire to socialize.

From high school onward, the emphasis on instruction needs to shift toward opportunities for the person to build on past experiences. Older learners tend to be much more discriminating; they want to know how information directly affects them, *why* they need to know something. Thus, it is imperative to present information that builds upon their experiences and anticipates their future needs. When working with older groups, museum staff and docents often worry that they will appear to be uninformed in comparison to their audience. The result is that presentations to these groups often grossly overestimate their interests and knowledge, although the opposite is also possible. If one provides mature groups an opportunity to express their interests and knowledge, one is far less likely to overshoot or undershoot the audience, and more likely to make them feel one really cares about their learning. Adults may not want to work in groups. When working with adult groups, it is best to let them suggest the length, social structure, and general content to be covered.

Social Context

4. **Organized trips are social events; visitors come accompanied by friends, teachers, and, often, family members.**

The social dynamics of organized trips are at once familiar to museum personnel and poorly understood. For example, it is noteworthy that most children who go on field trips can more easily, years later, remember the individuals with whom they went on the field trip than the experiences they encountered there.[10]

Some visitors socialize and affiliate in response to the discomfort they experience as a result of being in an unfamiliar museum setting.[11] Many visitors find museums uncomfortable places to visit. Museums need to develop programming that encourages socializing, for there is strong evidence that this creates a personal comfort zone that enables visitors to learn.

As we noted earlier, there is increasing evidence that children learn well together.[12] Models of cooperative learning are being developed in classrooms, and more and more students will be comfortable with cooperative learning when they arrive at the museum. For student groups, museums should try to devise ways for students to work on projects together, have them solve problems in groups, and then come together to share their solutions. Allow them opportunities to talk about what they are seeing and share ideas with their peers. This is difficult for very young children, but an excellent mode for older students. Ever mindful of diverse learning styles, it is probably wise to structure some learning experiences that accommodate those students who prefer learning alone.

5. Museum professionals have a tremendous impact on the quality of the museum experience.

Personal interaction increases the likelihood that a museum experience will be memorable.[13] A staff person can, and should, attempt to personalize the experience for each visitor. In our studies of children's recollections of school field trips, for example, we found it is not uncommon for children to remember qualities of docents or staff years after the experience.[14]

This human dimension can be used to advantage in programming. Having docents wear period dress, carry props, or assume roles can enhance the program and the chances that visitors will remember important concepts and ideas. It is also important to treat each visitor as an individual. Giving each person a little attention, making her or him feel special and important, almost guarantees that the museum experience will be both positive and memorable. No amount of mimeographed work sheets or self-guided tours will do this. People, especially well-trained and committed people, are still the key to high-quality education.

Physical Context

6. **Although some group leaders will plan a trip to see one particular collection or exhibition, most group members will want to see the whole museum.**

When visitors are told that they will be looking at just a small part of the museum, nothing will persuade them that they are not missing something. Despite the obvious pedagogic advantages of concentrating attention on a single exhibition or topic, most visitors, especially children, still want to see everything. Before the trip, visitors can be told that they will have an opportunity to spend a brief time seeing the whole museum, but first they will concentrate on a selected section. Results of research done on children suggest that this approach greatly facilitates all kinds of learning.[15] Also, recollection research suggests that many children are frustrated by not being able to look at the things they wanted to look at.

It is important to emphasize here that perception is more important than reality. What visitors need to know is that they will be given an opportunity to explore the whole institution at their own pace, looking at what they want to look at. It may not be possible to see everything in one visit, and they might have to come back; what is important is that they have the freedom to explore, and that the museum has explicitly acknowledged the legitimacy of their desire to "see everything."

7. **For many visitors, a changed attitude is the major outcome of an organized museum visit.**

Although the research on school field trips is equivocal about concept learning, it is unequivocal about attitudes.[16] Recollection research, as well as more traditional short-term studies, have consistently documented the strong feelings engendered by school field trips; these feelings are not

always positive ones. Although school field trips are perceived by the overwhelming majority of children as fun,
there are also many children who remember being fright-
ened or "feeling very small." It is important to remember
that the physical settings of museums can seem big, dark,
and imposing. Anything that can be done to help alleviate
visitors' anxieties in museum spaces, including just acknowledging their fears, can help them come away from the trip
with a positive feeling about the institution and improved
attitudes about the subject matter presented during the trip.
This can be as simple as providing easy-to-follow museum
plans, or placing museum staff so as to maximize their ability to assist visitors. Even when visitors can remember little
else about a museum trip, they can recall a general sense of
pleasure or discomfort.

Museums have focused on trying to teach content,
rather than exploring ways of maximizing the affective potential of visitors. A provocative conclusion developed by
Birney was that "structured" field trips resulted in superior
factual knowledge among participants, but that "unstructured" field trips yielded greater interest and enthusiasm for
the subject that was presented, that is, more positive attitudes.[17] Perhaps trying to find the balance between the structured and unstructured trip is the key.

8. **Many museums present such a wealth of stimuli that
   visitors may suffer from sensory overload.**
   Unable to use the controlling filters that most adults
apply in these situations, children often become hyperstimu-
lated. They run from one exhibit to the next, unable to focus
their attention on any one thing for longer than a few seconds. Telling children to slow down and concentrate on one
thing at a time is rarely a useful strategy. Pre-trip orientation
materials can help prepare children, but a more successful
strategy is to give children fifteen or twenty minutes to explore the setting at their own pace. For most children, this
initial exploratory period will significantly reduce these novelty and sensory overload effects. An even better approach
is to plan more than one field trip for a group so that, on the

second trip, children will be calmer and better able to focus on selected exhibits or objects.

As we noted earlier, most individuals can deal only with seven, plus or minus two, bits of information at a time, regardless of intelligence. What distinguishes experts from novices is the expert's ability to organize numerous bits of data into a chunk of information, based on previous knowledge and experience. For many visitors, each part of the museum is a separate chunk of information, a case of seeing the trees but not the forest. Inexperienced museum visitors, including most children, do not perceive a hall full of exhibits; they do not perceive a tropical reef ecosystem; they perceive a tank with hundreds of brightly colored individual fish, big fish, small fish, and some other things that are not fish. Helping visitors organize this information into larger chunks is an important component of the organized trip, and, to be successful, the educator must know where the learner is starting from.

****

The principles described in this chapter and the previous one are suggestions for ways that the Interactive Experience Model could be used as an organizing framework for the exhibition and program planning process. We have provided some of our own thoughts on what the implications of these principles might be. This model is new, but we have found it useful in preliminary testing. The real test will be its ability to help improve museum experiences.

Appendix

The following is the transcript of interviews of six members of a family that had visited the Museum of Natural History in London as a group.

The Interviews One year later, during the summer of 1986, six of the seven (Bill, Jane, Anne, Nan, Matt, and Bob) were together again. Five of the group were interviewed about their recollections of their visit to the Natural History Museum the previous summer. Two years later, Jill, the seventh member of the group, was also interviewed. None of the individuals interviewed had prior knowledge that they were going to be interviewed. None of the seven knew that the others had been, or were about to be, interviewed.

Bob

Q: Remember last summer when you were in England, you went to a museum. Who did you go with?
A: Nan, Anne, Grand Nanny (Nan), Matt, Dad (Bill), Jane, and me.
Q: What did the building look like?
A: It was a brick building, big, grayish in color. I remember walking up steps.
Q: What was the first thing you saw?
A: I remember seeing the bones of the big Brontosaurus [Diplodocus] and some of the dinosaurs. There was a little corner place that had all these little bones in them.
Q: Where did you go next?
A: The bathroom.
Q: What did the bathroom look like?
A: The bathroom was square, sort-of medium sized. There was a hallway, with things pointing to the men's and girl's bathroom.
Q: Then what did you do?

A: I went around the museum with Dad and Jane, and Nan, Anne, and Grand Nanny.

Q: Tell me all the things you remember seeing.

A: I remember seeing some dinosaur scenes. The skull of a saber-tooth tiger. The hair of a wooly mammoth (Was that in England? Yea, it was in England!).

Q: Did you eat anything?

A: I think we had lunch before. Oh, I remember now, we ate outside. I think we all ate yogurt. We played outside for a few minutes. The building was tall—it had two floors, it had windows.

Q: What else do you remember seeing at the museum?

A: Tyrannosaurus Rex. Elasmosaurus. A dinosaur with bumps on his head so he can breathe out of the top.

Q: Anything else?

A: We bought Lynn [younger sister not on the trip to London] a Triceratops—it was on the second floor where I got my Elasmosauraus too. Matt got that yellow guy, an Iquanodon.

We got postcards too. I can't remember what Grand Nanny bought at the gift shop, but she bought something.

Q: Anything else?

A: No.

Q: How long did you spend at the museum?

A: Maybe we were inside the museum an hour and a half. Everyone was ready to leave a long time before Daddy got done.

Matt

Q: Remember last summer when you were in England, you went to a museum. Who did you go with?

A: I went with Dad (Bill), Jane, and Donald Crumm [an English relative of Jane who Matt spent a lot of time with, but who was not part of the museum trip].

Q: What did the building look like?

A: It was a big building with dinosaur bones in it. It had those big black rocks [outside] that I wanted to climb on, like moon rocks.

Q: What was the first thing you saw?
A: Some kind of animal.
Q: What else did you see?
A: They had birds, fake birds, they were stuffed, pretty much a lot of them. I can't remember any ones in particular. They had mammals, they were stuffed too, both big ones and small ones. I think there were wolves. There were fish, wax fish. I saw fake whales, blue [whale], I think, humpbacked . . . those are the only two I can remember.
Q: Did you see anything else?
A: Yea, I saw a stuffed [saber-tooth tiger] and bones of a saber-tooth tiger, mastodon, mammoth, and wooly rhinoceros.
Q: Where did you have lunch?
A: We had lunch in the basement.
Q: Anything else?
A: No.
Q: How long did you spend in the museum?
A: I'm not sure, maybe an hour or two.

Anne

Q: Remember last summer when you were in England, you went to a museum. Who did you go with?
A: Nan, Jill, Jane, Bill, and the two boys [Bob and Matt].
Q: Tell me what you can remember. How did you get there?
A: We met Bill, Jane, Bob, and Matt at the subway station. Then we walked into the museum, all of us were there. We watched the boys for Bill, because he had a meeting.
Q: What did you see in the museum?
A: It was a hassle as to what we were going to see; there was such a myriad of choices. The boys wanted to see dinosaurs.

Mom [Nan] was restricted [difficulty walking]. We left Mom sitting in the foyer whilst we walked to various exhibits. Jill sat downstairs with Nan for a while. Jane and I and the boys went wandering through the museum.

I relived an experience, in the large open area with the banisters, I had a fear of the railing. Upstairs, I had a fear of the heights.

I can't remember any exhibits. All the various exhibits intermingle in my mind. There was a large elephant in the middle of the museum, I think [actually seen the previous summer with Jane at the National Museum of Natural History in Washington, D.C.].
Q: Did you eat anything?
A: Was that the day we picnicked outside? Yes, we had cheese, fruit, and bread. We may have done that before we went inside, but I don't believe so.

Then we met Bill again, and we probably went into the gift shop to look at books. After that we had lunch.
Q: Can you remember anything else?
A: No. I can't pick out even one thing that I remember seeing.
Q: How long did you spend at the museum?
A: I think it was about an hour and a half.

Nan

Q: Remember last summer when you were in England, you went to a museum. Who did you go with?
A: Went with Anne and Jill, also Bill, Jane, and the two boys [Bob and Matt].
Q: Tell me about the visit.
A: We were staying at Paula's house [Nan's niece]. Anne, Jill, and I took the bus, it took quite awhile. We went to the Beefeater stand at the Tower of London, we went to Buckingham Palace, the Cathedral, Regent's Park, then we went to the Natural History Museum. We all had lunch together. I can't remember where we met Bill, Jane, Bob, and Matt.
Q: What did you have for lunch?
A: A piece of cheese, or two, a crust of bread, and a Coke to drink. We also had ice cream.
Q: What did you do and see in the museum?
A: We went into the museum, I had been there when I was a little girl. We went up the stairs. There was so much to see. I said I was getting tired. What a nice place it was. We were there an hour or more, must have been. I can't remember anything I saw.

I bought a couple of little gifts for Andrew, Mark, and maybe Sue [grandchildren]. I bought Andrew a bookmark. I don't remember what I bought for Mark or Carol [Mark's wife]. I bought Sue a book all about museums.

Q: Anything else?

A: After the museum, we took Jill around Hyde Park. We pointed out things that George [relative], Michael [Anne's husband], and Anne used to do. Then we went to Trafalgar Square.

Jane

Q: Remember last summer when you were in England, you went to a museum. Who did you go with?

A: We (Matt, Bob, Bill, and I) met Jill, Mom (Anne), and Nan at the Tube, then we decided to get some stuff for lunch. It was a bright, sunny day. Bill took us to some little shops right by the museum that he remembered from when he worked there. We split up. We found a nice fruit shop and cheese shop. Bill went to the bakery and bought some bread and sweets. We had wine, Bill bought Nan an unusual soda that she adored. We ate a luxurious picnic on the grounds of the museum. Bob tried to throw away a peach without eating it, which caused a fuss.

We went into the museum. Bill had that meeting. We split up.

Matt and I walked through some animal hall—prehistoric animals. He was thrilled, later he took Anne and Jill through it. I stayed out with Nan at that point.

Matt was having an absolute fit about the order in which we saw things. Bob sat down with Nan and me, he was bored.

Bob asked how long Diplodocus was. We measured it in "Bob feet"—we spent a lot of time at this. Matt did it too.

Mom (Anne) went to the bathroom. She came back all excited because the toilet paper was just like the stuff they used after the war—that cellophaney toilet paper.

Then Bill came back. Matt wanted to show Bill the prehistoric animal [mammal] exhibit.

Then we did the gift shops.

Didn't Bill go over to see if the guy in the umbrella stand was still there? He did, but the guy didn't remember him.

Q: What did you do when you first walked into the museum?

A: We walked directly into the main hall. Matt and Bob were enthralled with the dinosaurs. Mom and Jill went upstairs.

At some point, Matt and I went to the right to the pre-historic mammals. I never went upstairs.

Q: What do you remember about prehistoric mammals?

A: Not a whole lot. Matt knew a lot of the animals. There were dioramas, big animals, tusks, fur—real traditional exhibits. The place had a musty smell. It was crowded that day.

Q: What kind of people were there in the museum?

A: I can't remember.

Q: Anything else you can remember?

A: There were lots of pigeons outside by our picnic.

I didn't buy anything at the gift shop. I was looking for a book for Bill. I can't remember what now. I think I looked at postcards too. I remember Nan bought something at the gift shop, but I can't remember what.

Q: How long did you spend at the museum?

A: Maybe we were inside the museum an hour and a half. Everyone was ready to leave a long time before Bill got done with his meeting.

Jill

Q: Remember when you were in England and you went to the Natural History Museum? Who did you go with?

A: Mom and Nan, Bill, Jane, and the boys. But I couldn't remember anything else, it was too long ago.

Q: Remember walking up the stairs and entering the museum? What did you see?

A: I remember being really struck by the architecture. The building was so big and beautiful.

Q: Do you remember what color it was or what material it was made out of?

A: No, but there were stained glass windows. I remember that. I remember the stairs, big beautiful stairs. I remember standing up at the top of them and waving to Nan, trying to get her attention. There was a big dinosaur in the middle of the room downstairs. I had never seen a building like that before.

Q: *Do you remember what was upstairs?*

A: No. There were two sets of stairs, but I can't remember anything else up there. I know I tried to get Mom to look out over the railing, but she was scared to get close to the edge. Standing on the upper level, I remember the light streaming through the windows down to the level below. It was a very beautiful sight.

Q: *When you walked into the museum, where did you go?*

A: I don't remember. I think we went and looked at dinosaurs.

The boys went running around the dinosaurs. I think we went to look at dinosaurs. I remember walking down a hallway, it was the hallway near the gift shop, and there were large glass cases filled with birds.

I can't remember much else, except eating lunch.

Q: *Tell me about lunch.*

A: We ate outside. There was a grassy area. I think we ate under a tree and there was a bench there.

Q: *What did you have for lunch?*

A: I remember we went to a bunch of small shops. I think we had cheese, some kind of meat, I think ham. That's all I can remember.

Q: *How long did you spend in the museum?*

A: I can't remember, maybe two or three hours.

References

Preface

1. Naisbitt, J., & Aburdene, P. (1990). *Megatrends 2000*. New York: Avon Books.
2. Ibid.

Introduction

1. Jaynes, J. (1976). The origin of consciousness in the breakdown of the bicameral mind. Boston: Houghton Mifflin.

Chapter 1

1. Parker, S. (1971). *The future of work and leisure*. New York: Praeger.
2. Balling, J. D., & Cornell, E. A. (1985). *Family visitors to science-technology centers: Motivations and demographics*. (Final Report Grant No. SED-8112927). Washington, DC: National Science Foundation.
3. Pollock, J. C., Finn, P., Garfield, E. A., Snyder, A., & Pfenning, A. G. (1983). *Where does the time go?* New York: The United Media Enterprise Report on Leisure in America.
4. Reit, S. V. (1981). In S. V. Radner (Ed.), *The pleasure of their company*. New York: Chilton.
5. Gudykunst, W. B., Morra, J. A., Kantor, W. I., & Parker, H. A. Dimensions of leisure activities: A factor analytic study in New England. *Journal of Leisure Research, 13*(1), 28–42.
6. Falk, J. H. (1992). *The utilization of science museums by African Americans*. Unpublished manuscript.
7. Falk, J. H. (1983). The use of time as a measure of visitor behavior and exhibit effectiveness. *Roundtable Reports, 7*(4), 10–13.
8. Gorr, L., Mahnken, M., Nordstrom, J., & Walls, D.

(1980). *A profile of visitors: The Dallas Museum of Natural History.* Unpublished manuscript, University of Dallas, Irving, TX.

Rosenfeld, S. (1980). *Informal learning in zoos: Naturalistic studies of family groups.* Unpublished doctoral dissertation, University of California, Berkeley.

Miles, R. S. (1986). Museum audiences. *The International Journal of Museum Management and Curatorship, 5*, 73–80.

9. Graburn, N. H. H. (1977, June). The museum and the visitor experience. In *The visitor and the museum* (pp. 5–32). Prepared for the 72nd Annual Conference of the American Association of Museums, Seattle, WA.

10. Gorr et al., *Profile of visitors,* 30–41.

Balling & Cornell, *Family visitors.*

Rosenfeld, *Informal learning.*

Miles, "Museum audiences," 73–80.

11. Adams, G. D. (1989). *The process and effects of word-of-mouth communication at a history museum.* Unpublished master's thesis, Boston University.

12. Rosenfeld, *Informal learning.*

13. Birney, B. (1986). *A comparative study of children's perceptions and knowledge of wildlife and conservation as they relate to field trip experiences at the Los Angeles County Museum of Natural History and the Los Angeles Zoo.* Unpublished doctoral dissertation, University of California at Los Angeles.

Kimche, L. (1978). Science centers: A potential for learning. *Science, 199*(20), 270–273.

Miles, "Museum audiences," 73–80.

14. Kellert, S. R. (1980). *Activities of the American public relating to animals, phase II* (Report No. PB80–194525). Arlington, VA: National Technical Information Service.

15. Borun, M. (1977). *Measuring the immeasurable: A pilot study of museum effectiveness.* Washington, DC: Association of Science-Technology Centers.

Adams, *Process and effects.*

16. Falk, *Utilization of science museums.*

17. Adams, *Process and effects.*

18. Graburn, "Museum and the visitor," 5–32.

19. Yellis, K. (1985). *Reverence, association, and education: Testing a typology of museum-goer needs.* Unpublished manuscript.

20. Newman, A. (1991). *Insights: Museums, visitors, attitudes and expectations.* Los Angeles: Getty Center for Education in the Arts.

21. Gudykunst et al., "Dimensions of leisure activities," 28–42.

22. Arnell, U., Hammer, I., & Nylöf, G. (1976). *Going to museums*. Stockholm: Riksutstallningar/Swedish Travelling Exhibitions.

Griggs, S. A., & Hays-Jackson, K. (1982). Visitors' perceptions of cultural institutions. *British Journal of Psychology, 73,* 121–125.

Hood, M. G. (1983). Staying away: Why people choose not to visit museums. *Museum News,* pp. 50–57.

23. Gudykunst et al., "Dimensions of leisure activities," 28–42.

24. Hood, M. G. (1981). *Leisure criteria of family participation and non-participation in museums.* Unpublished manuscript, Hood Associates, Columbus, OH.

25. Ibid.

26. Adams, *Process and effects.*

27. U.S. Bureau of the Census. (1985). *Statistical abstract of the United States* (105th ed.). Washington, DC: U.S. Department of Commerce.

28. Naisbitt & Aburdene, *Megatrends 2000.*

29. Arnell, Hammer, & Nylöf, *Going to museums.*

Hood, "Staying away," 50–57.

Gudykunst et al., "Dimensions of leisure activities," 28–42.

Balling & Cornell, *Family visitors.*

Duncan, D. J. (1978). Leisure types: Factor analyses of leisure profiles. *Journal of Leisure Research, 10,* 113–125.

Cheek, N. H., Field, D. R., & Burdge, R. (1976). *Leisure and recreation places.* Ann Arbor, MI: Ann Arbor Science Publications.

30. Miles, "Museum audiences," 73–80.

31. Hood, "Staying away," 50–57.

Morris, R. E. (1968). Leisure time and the museum. In S. F. deBorhegyi & I. A. Hanson (Eds.), *The museum visitor.* Milwaukee, WI: Milwaukee Public Museum, Publications in Museology.

Newman, *Insights: Museums.*

32. Balling & Cornell, *Family visitors.*

Morris, "Leisure time."

Bigman, S. K. (1956). Art exhibit audiences. *Museologist, 59,* 2–18, and *60,* 2–6.

33. Adams, *Process and effects.*

Alt, M. B. (1980). Four years of visitor surveys at the British Museum (Natural History) 1976–1979. *Museum Journal, 80,* 10–19.

Arnell, Hammer, & Nylöf, *Going to museums.*

Cheek, Field, & Burdge, *Leisure and recreation places.*

Kwong, M. (1977). *Lion/tiger area observation.* Unpublished manuscript, National Zoological Park, Washington, DC.

Bigman, "Art exhibit audiences," 2–18, 2–6.

deBorhegyi, S. F., & Hanson, I. A. (1966). *Chronological bibliography of museum visitor surveys* (pp. 239–251). Washington, DC: American Association of Museums.

Borun, *Measuring the immeasurable.*

Balling & Cornell, *Family visitors.*

Wolf, R. L., & Tymitz, B. L. (1978). *Whatever happened to the giant wombat: An investigation of the impact of the "Ice Age Mammals and Emergence of Man" exhibit, National Museum of Natural History.* Washington, DC: Smithsonian Institution.

Wolf, R. L., & Tymitz, B. L. (1979). *"Do giraffes ever sit?": A study of visitor perceptions at the National Zoological Park, Smithsonian Institution.* Washington, DC: Smithsonian Institution.

Wolf, R. L., & Tymitz, B. L. (1979). *East side, west side, straight down the middle: A study of visitor perceptions of "Our Changing Land," the bicentennial exhibit, National Museum of Natural History.* Washington, DC: Smithsonian Institution.

Wolf, R. L., & Tymitz, B. L. (1980). *"When will the fourth floor be open?": A study of visitor perceptions of the Hirshhorn Museum and Sculpture Garden.* Washington, DC: Smithsonian Institution.

Wolf, R. L., & Tymitz, B. L. (1981). *"Hey Mom, that exhibit's alive": A study of visitor perceptions of the coral reef exhibit, National Museum of Natural History.* Washington, DC: Smithsonian Institution.

Kuehl, P. G. (1976). *An analysis of visitor socioeconomic, behavioral, and attitudinal characteristics at the National Zoological Park. Final Report for the National Zoological Park, Washington, DC.* Unpublished manuscript.

National Research Center for the Arts. (1973). *Arts and the people: A survey of public attitudes and participation in the arts and culture of New York State.* New York: Publishing Center for Cultural Resources, American Council for the Arts in Education.

Association of Science-Technology Centers. (1976). *Survey of members.* Washington, DC: Author.

34. Kelly, J. R. (1977). Leisure socialization: Replication and extension. *Journal of Leisure Research, 9,* 121–132.

35. Adams, *Process and effects.*

Alt, "Visitor surveys," 10–19.

Arnell, Hammer, & Nylöf, *Going to museums.*

Wolf & Tymitz, *Whatever happened to the giant wombat.*

Wolf & Tymitz, *When will the fourth floor be open?*

Cheek, Field, & Burdge, *Leisure and recreation places.*

Walker, E. (1988). A front-end evaluation conducted to facilitate planning the Royal Ontario Museum's European galleries. In S. Bitgood, J. Roper, Jr., & A. Benefield (Eds.), *Visitor studies— 1988: Theory, research, and practice. Proceedings of the First Annual Visitor Studies Conference* (pp. 139–148). Jacksonville, AL: The Center for Social Design.

36. Arnell, Hammer, & Nylöf, *Going to museums.*

37. Walker, "Front-end evaluation," 139–148.

38. American Museum of Natural History. (1989, 1990). *Visitor surveys.* Unpublished manuscripts.

Maryland Science Center. (1990). *Visitor surveys.* Unpublished manuscript.

Falk, J. H. (n.d.). *Visitor surveys,* Unpublished manuscript.

39. Falk, *Utilization of science museums.*

40. American Association of Museums. (1992). *Excellence and equity: Education and the public dimension. Report from AAM's Task Force on Museum Education.* Washington, DC: Author.

41. Hood, M. G. (1988). Arboretum visitor profiles as defined by the four seasons. In S. Bitgood, J. Roper, Jr., & A. Benefield (Eds.), *Visitor studies—1988: Theory, research, and practice. Proceedings of the First Annual Visitor Studies Conference.* (pp. 84–100). Jacksonville, AL: The Center for Social Design.

42. Ibid., 84–100.

43. Ibid., 84–100.

Chapter 2

1. Adams, *Process and effects.*

Kimche, "Science centers," 270–273.

Rosenfeld, S. (1979). The context of informal learning in zoos. *Museum Education Roundtable, Roundtable Reports, 4*(2), 1–3, 15–16.

Falk, J. H., Balling, J. D., & Liversidge, J. *Family visitors to the National Zoological Park: A look at agendas.* Unpublished manuscript.

Balling & Cornell, *Family visitors.*

2. Griggs, S. A. (1990). Perceptions of traditional versus new style exhibitions at the Natural History Museum. *ILVS Review: A Journal of Visitor Behavior, 1*(2), 78–90.2.

3. Taylor, S. (1991, June). *How do you define a successful family experience?* Address to the Museum Education Roundtable/Virginia Museums Association Conference on Families in Museums, Fairfax, VA.

4. Griggs, "Perceptions of exhibitions," 78–90.2.

5. Adams, *Process and effects.*

6. Kelly, "Leisure socialization," 121–132.

7. Hood, "Staying away," 50–57.

8. Loomis, R. J. (1987). *Museum visitor evaluation: New tool for management* (p. 123). Nashville, TN: American Association for State and Local History.

9. Adams, *Process and effects.*

10. Ibid.

11. Borun, *Measuring the immeasurable.*

Slowik, P. (1980). *Brandywine River Museum visitor survey, July 9–August 11, 1980.* Unpublished manuscript.

Slowik, P. *The Conner Prairie Pioneer Settlement, August 1982 and August 1986.* Unpublished manuscript.

Bitgood, S., Patterson, D., & Nichols, G. (1986). *Report of a survey of visitors to the Anniston Museum of Natural History.* Jacksonville, AL: Jacksonville State University, Psychology Institute.

Survey of Biltmore Estate, Summer 1987. Unpublished manuscript.

Survey of Museums at Stony Brook, 1976 to 1984, 1987, 1988. Unpublished manuscripts.

Survey of Colonial Michilimakinac. (1988). Unpublished manuscript.

12. Roper, G. (1988). Roper poll. *Social Science Monitor, 10*(4), 2.

13. Katz, E., & Lazarsfeld, P. F. (1955). *Personal influence: The part played by people in the flow of mass communication.* Glencoe, MN: The Free Press.

14. Arndt, J. (1967). *Word-of-mouth advertising.* New York: Advertising Research Foundation.

15. Adams, *Process and effects.*

16. Balling, J. D., Falk, J., & Aronson, R. (1992). *Pre-trip orientations: An exploration of their effects on learning from a single visit field trip to a zoological park.* Manuscript submitted for publication.

17. Ausubel, D. P. (1960). The use of advance organizers in the learning and retention of meaningful verbal material. *Journal of Educational Psychology, 41,* 267–272.

Screven, C. G. (1986). Educational exhibitions: Some areas for controlled research. *Journal of Museum Education, 11*(1), 7–11.

Screven, C. G. (1986). Exhibitions and information centers: Some principles and approaches. *Curator, 29*(2), 109–137.

18. Balling, Falk, & Aronson, *Pre-trip orientations.*

19. Ibid.

20. Falk, J. H. & Balling, J. D. (1992). *The role of context in facilitating learning.* Manuscript submitted for publication.

21. Falk, J. H., Balling, J. D. & Liversidge, J. (1985). *Information and agenda: Strategies for enhancing the educational value of family visits to a zoological park.* (Interim Report, Scholarly Studies No. 1231S4–01). Washington, DC: Smithsonian Institution.

22. Dierking, L. D. (1987). *Parent-child interactions in a free choice learning setting: An examination of attention directing behavior.* Unpublished doctoral dissertation, University of Florida, Gainesville, FL.

23. Falk, J. H. (1989). [Investigations of visitors to natural history museums]. Unpublished raw data.

24. Rosenfeld, "Context of informal learning," 1–3, 15–16.

Adams, *Process and effects.*

Balling & Cornell, *Family visitors.*

25. Hood, "Staying away," 50–57.

Chapter 3

1. Lakota, R. A. (1975). *The National Museum of Natural History as a behavioral environment—Part I—Book I.* (Final Report). Washington, DC: Smithsonian Institution, Office of Museum Programs.

Rosenfeld, *Informal learning.*

Diamond, J. (1979). *The social behavior of adult-child groups in the science museum.* Unpublished doctoral dissertation, University of California, Berkeley.

Dierking, *Parent-child interactions.*

Falk, J. H. (1991). Analysis of the behavior of family visitors in history museums: The National Museum of Natural History. *Curator, 34*(1), 44–50.

Falk, J. H., Koran, J. J., Dierking, L. D., & Dreblow, L. (1985). Predicting visitor behavior. *Curator, 28*, 249–257.

Hilke, D. D., & Balling, J. D. (1985). *The family as a learning system: An observational study of family behavior in an information rich environment.* (Final Report Grant No.: SED-812927). Washington, DC: National Science Foundation.

   Snow-Dockser, L. (1987). *Parent-child interaction in a children's museum: The interrelated dynamics of the informal learning environment.* Paper presented at the Seventeenth Annual Symposium of the Jean Piaget Society. Boston, MA.

   2. Rosenfeld, *Informal learning.*

   3. Silverman, L. (1990). *Of us and other "things": The content and functions of talk by adult visitor pairs in an art and history museum.* Unpublished doctoral dissertation, University of Pennsylvania.

   4. Balling & Cornell, *Family visitors.*

   Borun, *Measuring the immeasurable.*

   McManus, P. (1987, June). It's the company you keep . . . The social determination of learning-related behavior in a science museum. *International Journal of Museum Management and Curatorship.*

   Taylor, S. (1986). *Understanding processes of informal education: A naturalistic study of visitors to a public aquarium.* Unpublished doctoral dissertation, University of California, Berkeley.

   Benton, D. P. (1979). *Intergenerational interaction in museums.* Unpublished doctoral dissertation, Columbia University Teacher's College, New York.

   Cone, C. A., & Kendall, K. (1978). Space, time and family interactions: Visitor behavior at the Science Museum of Minnesota. *Curator, 21,* 245–258.

   Diamond, *Social behavior.*

   Lakota, *National Museum of Natural History.*

   Dierking, *Parent–child interactions.*

   Rosenfeld, *Informal learning.*

   Hilke & Balling, *Family as a learning system.*

   Wolf & Tymitz, *Do giraffes ever sit?*

   Rosenfeld, "Context of informal learning," 1–3, 15–16.

   5. Lakota, *National Museum of Natural History.*

   6. Diamond, *Social behavior.*

   7. Koran, J. J., Jr., & Koran, M. L. (1984). The roles of attention and curiosity in museum learning. In S. K. Nichols, M. Alexander, & K. Yellis (Eds.), *Museum education anthology: Perspectives on informal learning* (pp. 205–213). Washington, DC: Museum Education Roundtable.

   Koran, J. J., Jr., Koran, M. L., & Longino, S. J. (1986). The relationship of age, sex, attention and holding power with two types of science exhibits. *Curator, 29,* 227–235.

Koran, J. J., Jr., Koran, M. L., Foster, J., & Dierking, L. D. (1988). Using modeling to direct attention. *Curator, 31*(1), 36–42.

8. Rosenfeld, *Informal learning.*

Rosenfeld, "Context of informal learning," 3–5.

9. Benton, *Intergenerational interaction.*

Bitgood, S. (1986). Variables influencing visitor behavior: Physical qualities of the exhibit object/species. *Visitor Behavior, 1*(1), 5.

Taylor, *Understanding processes of informal education.*

Wolf & Tymitz, *Do giraffes ever sit?*

10. Diamond, *Social behavior.*

Rosenfeld, *Informal learning.*

McManus, "It's the company you keep."

11. McManus, "It's the company you keep."

Rosenfeld, *Informal learning.*

12. Dierking, L. D. (1989). The family museum experience: Implications from research. *Journal of Museum Education, 14*(2), 9–11.

Dierking, L. D., Koran, J. J., Jr., Koran, M. L., & Falk, J. H. (1992). *Family behavior in free choice learning settings: A review of the research.* Manuscript submitted for publication.

13. Benton, *Intergenerational interaction.*

14. Taylor, *Understanding processes of informal education.*

15. Hensel, K. (1987). *Families in a museum: Interactions and conversations at displays.* Unpublished doctoral dissertation, Columbia University Teacher's College, New York.

16. Snow–Dockser, *Parent-child interaction.*

Snow–Dockser, L. (1987). Family interviews in a play exhibit. *Journal of Museum Education, 12*(1), 17–18.

17. Taylor, *Successful family experience.*

18. Dierking, *Parent–child interactions.*

Hilke & Balling, *Family as a learning system.*

19. Falk et al., "Predicting visitor behavior," 249–257.

Falk, "Analysis of the behavior of family," 44–50.

20. Falk, J. H. (n.d.). [Observations of families at the National Museum of Natural History, Smithsonian Institution]. Unpublished raw data.

21. Falk et al., "Predicting visitor behavior," 249–257.

Falk, "Analysis of the behavior of family," 44–50.

22. McManus, P. (1989). Oh yes, they do: How museum visitors read labels and interact with exhibit text. *Curator, 32*(3), 174–180.

23. McManus, "It's the company you keep."

24. Bandura, A., & Walters, R. (1963). *Social learning and personality development.* New York: Holt, Rinehart and Winston.

25. Birney, *Comparative study of children's perceptions.*

Martin, W. W., Falk, J. H., & Balling, J. D. (1981). Environmental effects on learning: The outdoor field trip. *Science Education,* 65(3), 301–309.

26. Birney, *Comparative study of children's perceptions.*

27. Falk, J. H., (1988). Museum recollections. In S. Bitgood, J. Roper, Jr., & A. Benefield (Eds.), *Visitor studies—1988: Proceedings of the First Annual Visitor Studies Conference* (pp. 60–65). Jacksonville, AL: The Center for Social Design.

Falk, J. H., & Dierking, L. D. (1991). The effect of visitation frequency on long term recollection. In S. Bitgood, A. Benefield, & D. Patterson (Eds.), *Visitor Studies: Theory, Research, and Practice* (Vol. 3, pp. 94–103). *Proceedings of the 1990 Visitor Studies Conference.* Jacksonville, AL: The Center for Social Design.

28. Falk, J. H., & Balling, J. D. (1982). The field trip milieu: Learning and behavior as a function of contextual events. *Journal of Educational Research,* 76(1), 22–28.

Falk, J. H., Martin, W. W., & Balling, J. D. (1978). The novel field trip phenomenon: Adjustment to novel settings interferes with task learning. *Journal of Research in Science Teaching, 15,* 468–472.

Falk, J. H. (1983). A cross-cultural investigation of the novel field trip phenomenon: National Museum of Natural History, New Delhi, India. *Curator, 26,* 315–325.

Martin, Falk, & Balling, "Environmental effects," 301–309.

29. Martin, Falk, & Balling, "Environmental effects," 301–309.

30. Schachter, S. (1959). *The psychology of affiliation.* Stanford, CA: Stanford University Press.

31. Hayward, D. G. (1980). *Visitor-oriented research at Old Sturbridge Village* (Research Report). Amherst, MA: University of Massachusetts, Environment and Behavior Research Center.

32. Birney, *Comparative study of children's perceptions.*

33. Falk, "Museum recollections," 60–65.

Falk & Dierking, "Effect of visitation frequency," 94–103.

34. Johnson, D. W., & Johnson, R. (1987). *Learning together and alone: Cooperation, competition, and individualization* (2nd ed.). Englewood Cliffs, NJ: Prentice-Hall.

35. Falk et al., "Predicting visitor behavior," 249–257.

Falk, "Analysis of the behavior of family," 44–50.
36. Rosenfeld, "Context of informal learning."
Koran et al., "Using modeling," 36–42.
37. Koran et al., "Using modeling," 36–42.
38. Koran, J. J., Jr. (1972). The use of modeling, feedback and practice variables to influence science teacher behavior. *Science Education, 56,* 285–291.
Koran et al., "Using modeling," 36–42.
39. Koran et al., "Using modeling," 36–42.
40. Falk et al., "Predicting visitor behavior," 249–256.
Falk, "Analysis of the behavior of family," 44–50.
41. Bandura & Walters, *Social learning.*
42. Rosenfeld, "Context of informal learning."
43. Falk, "Museum recollections," 60–65.
Falk & Dierking, "Effect of visitation frequency," 94–103.

Chapter 4

1. Gilman, B. I. (1916). Museum fatigue. *Science Monthly, 12,* 62–74.
2. Robinson, E. S. (1931). Psychological studies of the public museum. *School and Society, 33,* 121–125.
3. Melton, A. (1935). Problems of installation in museums of art. *AAM Monograph* (New Series No. 14).
Melton, A. (1933). Studies of installation at the Pennsylvania Museum of Art. *Museum News, 10*(15), 5–8.
Melton, A. W., Feldman, N. G., & Mason, C. W. (1936). *Experimental studies of the education of children in a museum of science.* Washington, DC: American Association of Museums.
Melton, A. W. (1972). Visitor behavior in museums: Some early research in environmental design. *Human Factors, 14*(5), 393–403.
4. Serrell, B. (1977). Survey of visitor attitude and awareness at an aquarium. *Curator, 20*(1), 48–52.
Falk et al., "Predicting visitor behavior," 249–257.
Falk, "Analysis of the behavior of family," 44–50.
5. Melton, "Problems of installation."
6. Porter, M. C. (1938). Behavior of the average visitor in the Peabody Museum of Natural History. *Yale University Publications of the American Association of Museums* (New Series, No. 16).
deBorhegyi, S. F. (1968). Testing of audience reaction to museum exhibits. In S. F. deBorhegyi & I. A. Hanson (Eds.), *The*

museum visitor. Milwaukee: Milwaukee Public Museum Publications in Museology.

Loomis, R. J., & Hummel, C. F. (1975). Observations and recommendations on visitor utilization problems of the Denver Museum of Natural History. *Working Papers in Visitor Studies* (No. 1).

Serrell, "Survey of visitor attitude," 48–52.

Taylor, *Understanding processes of informal education.*

7. Melton, "Problems of installation."

8. Nielson, L. C. (1946). A technique for studying the behavior of museum visitors. *Journal of Educational Psychology, 37,* 103–110.

9. Allen, P., & Shacklett, A. (1982). *Epcot Center computer simulation model.* Unpublished manuscript, WED Industries, Inc.

Falk et al., "Predicting visitor behavior," 249–257.

10. Falk et al., "Predicting visitor behavior," 249–257.

Falk, "Analysis of the behavior of family," 44–50.

11. Falk, Martin, & Balling, "Novel field trip phenomenon," 468–472.

Martin, Falk, & Balling, "Environmental effects," 301–309.

Falk & Balling, "Field trip milieu," 22–28.

Falk, "Cross-cultural investigation," 315–325.

12. Falk, Martin, & Balling, "Novel field trip phenomenon," 468–472.

Martin, Falk, & Balling, "Environmental effects," 301–309.

13. Falk, Martin, & Balling, "Novel field trip phenomenon," 468–472.

Falk & Balling, "Field trip milieu," 22–28.

Falk, "Cross-cultural investigation," 315–325.

Balling, Falk, & Aronson, "Pre-trip orientations."

14. Falk et al., "Predicting visitor behavior," 249–257.

Falk, "Analysis of the behavior of family," 44–50.

15. Nielson, "A technique for studying," 103–110.

Diamond, *Social behavior.*

Taylor, *Understanding processes of informal education.*

16. Hayward, D. G. & Brydon-Miller, M. L. (1984). Spatial and conceptual aspects of orientation: Visitor experiences at an outdoor history museum. *Journal of Environmental Systems, 13*(4), 317–332.

17. Lynch, K. (1960). *The Image of the City.* Cambridge, MA: MIT Press.

Gould, P., & White, R. (1974). *Mental Maps.* London: Penguin.

Robinson, A., & Petchenick, B. (1976). *The nature of maps:*

Essays towards understanding maps and mapping. Chicago: University of Chicago Press.

   Stea, D. (1976). Program notes on a spatial fugue. In G. T. Moore & R. G. Golledge (Eds.), *Environmental knowing.* Stroudsburg, PA: Dowden, Hutchinson, and Ross.

   Winkler, R. (1970). *Use of maps and guides at the National Museum of History and Technology.* Unpublished manuscript, Smithsonian Institution, Washington, DC.

   Morris, R. G. M., & Alt, M. B. (1979). An experiment to help design a map for a large museum. *Museum Journal,* 179–180.

18. Koran et al., "Using modeling," 36–42.

19. Melton, "Visitor behavior in museums," 393–403.

20. deBorhegyi, "Testing of audience reaction."

21. Hilgard, E. R., & Bower, G. H. (1966). *Theories of learning* (3rd ed.). New York: Appleton-Century-Crofts.

   Bransford, J. D. (1979). *Human cognition: Learning, understanding and remembering.* Belmont, CA: Wadsworth.

22. Falk, "Use of time," 10–13.

23. Falk, J. H. (1989). *Understanding audience behavior and learning: Lessons from "Engines of Change" and "After the Revolution."* Unpublished manuscript, National Museum of American History, Washington, DC.

24. Falk, "Analysis of the behavior of family," 44–50.

   Dierking, *Parent-child interactions.*

25. Falk et al., "Predicting visitor behavior," 249–257.

   Falk, "Analysis of the behavior of family," 44–50.

   Hayward & Brydon-Miller, "Spatial and conceptual aspects of orientation," 317–332.

   Balling, Falk, & Aronson, "Pre-trip orientations."

26. Barker, R. G. (1968). *Ecological psychology.* Palo Alto, CA: Stanford University Press.

   Barker, R. G. & Wright, H. F. (1955). *Midwest and its children.* New York: Harper and Row.

27. Barker & Wright, *Midwest.*

28. Wicker, A. W. (1979). *An introduction to ecological psychology.* Monterey, CA: Brooks/Cole.

29. Falk et al., "Predicting visitor behavior," 249–257.

   Falk, "Analysis of the behavior of family," 44–50.

30. Koran et al., "Using modeling," 36–42.

31. Ibid., 36–42.

32. Nahemov, L. (1971). Research in a novel environment. *Environment and Behavior, 3,* 81–102.

33. deBorhegyi, "Testing of audience reaction," 23–25.

Abler, T. (1968). Traffic pattern and exhibit design: A study of learning in the museum. In S. F. deBorhegyi & I. A. Hanson (Eds.), *The museum visitor* (pp. 104–119). Milwaukee: Milwaukee Public Museum Publications in Museology.

34. Cohen, R. (Ed.). (1985). *The development of spatial cognition.* Hillsdale, NJ: Lawrence Erlbaum.

Evans, G. W. (1980). Environmental cognition. *Psychological Bulletin, 88,* 259–287.

Liben, L. S., Patterson, A. H., & Newcombe, N. (Eds.). (1981). *Spatial representation and behavior across the lifespan: Theory and application.* New York: Academic Press.

Mandler, J . M. (1983). Representation. In J. H. Flavell & E. M. Markman (Eds.), *Handbook of child psychology* (Vol. 3). New York: John Wiley.

Lynch, *Image of the city.*

35. Falk, J. H. & Rowe, M. B., (n.d.). *Cognitive maps: The consolidation of memories from the Florida Museum of Natural History.* Unpublished manuscript.

Chapter 5

1. Neal, A. (1976). *Exhibits for the small museum: A handbook.* Nashville, TN: American Association for State and Local History.

Serrell, B. (1983). *Making exhibit labels: A step-by- step guide.* Nashville, TN: American Association for State and Local History.

Flesh, R. (1962). *The art of readable writing.* New York: Macmillan.

McLendon, C., & Blackstone, M. (1982). *Signage.* New York: McGraw-Hill.

Loomis, *Museum visitor evaluation.*

Screven, "Exhibitions and information centers," 109–137.

Bitgood, S., & Gregg, G. (1986). A brief review of the research on signs and labels: Where are the data? *Visitor Behavior, 1*(3), 4.

Borun, M. (1980). To label or not to label. *Museum News, 58*(4), 64–67.

Miles, R. S., Alt, M. B., Gosling, D. C., Lewis, B. N., & Tout, A. F. (Eds.) (1982). *The design of educational exhibits.* London: George Allen and Unwin.

2. Melton, "Problems of installation."

Melton, "Visitor behavior in museums."

Porter, "Behavior of the average of visitor."

Screven, C. G. (1969). The museum as a responsive learning environment. *Museum News, 47*(10), 7–10.

Screven, C. G. (1976). Exhibit evaluation: A goal-referenced approach. *Curator, 19*(4), 281–282.

Shettel, H. H. (1973). Exhibits: Art form or educational medium? *Museum News, 52*(9), 32–41.

Shettel, H. H., Butcher, M., Cotton, T., Northrup, J., & Slough, D. C. (1968). *Strategies for determining exhibit effectiveness* (Tech. Rep. No. AIR-E59–4/68-FR). Pittsburgh, PA: American Institute for Research.

3. Falk et al., "Predicting visitor behavior," 249–257.

Falk, *Understanding audience behavior and learning.*

Falk, "Analysis of the behavior of family," 44–50.

4. Falk et al., "Predicting visitor behavior," 249–257.

Falk, "Analysis of the behavior of family," 44–50.

5. Falk, *Understanding audience behavior and learning.*

6. Bitgood, "Variables influencing visitor behavior," 5.

7. Melton, "Visitor behavior in museums," 393–403.

Screven, "Museum as a responsive learning environment," 7–10.

Shettel, "Exhibits: Art form or educational," 32–41.

8. Shettel, H. (1968). An evaluation of existing criteria for judging the quality of science exhibits. *Curator, 11*(2), 137–153.

Shettel, "Exhibits: Art form or educational," 32–41.

9. Munley, M. E. (1982). *Telltale tools.* Unpublished manuscript, Smithsonian Institution, National Museum of American History, Washington, DC.

10. Bitgood, S., Patterson, D., & Benefield, A. (1986). *Understanding your visitors: Ten factors that influence visitor behavior* (Tech. Rep. No. 86–60). Jacksonville, AL: Psychology Institute.

11. Falk, "Use of Time," 10–13.

Borun, M., & Miller, M. (1980). *What's in a name?* Philadelphia: The Franklin Institute Science Museum.

Screven, C. G. (1974). *The measurement and facilitation of learning in the museum environment: An experimental analysis.* Washington, DC: Smithsonian Institution Press.

Laetsch, W. M. (1982). An overview of research on museum visitors. In J. Glaser (Ed.), *Proceedings of "Children in Museums: An International Symposium."* Washington, DC: Smithsonian Institution.

12. Ibid.

13. Falk et al., "Predicting visitor behavior," 249–257.

Falk, "Analysis of the behavior of family," 44–50.

14. McManus, "Oh yes, they do," 174–180.

15. Bechtel, R. B. (1967). Hodometer research in museums. *Museum News, 45*(3), 23–26.

16. Wolf & Tymitz, "Whatever happened to the giant wombat."

17. Falk et al., "Predicting visitor behavior," 249–257.

Falk, "Analysis of the behavior of family," 44–50.

18. Diamond, *Social Behavior.*

19. Borun & Miller, *What's in a name?*

20. Dierking, *Parent-child interactions.*

21. Hilke & Balling, *Family as a learning system.*

McManus, "Oh yes, they do," 174–180.

22. Diamond, *Social behavior.*

23. Hilke & Balling, *Family as a learning system.*

24. Lawson, A., Karplus, R., & Ali, H. (1978). The acquisition of propositional logic and formal operational schemata during secondary school years. *Journal of Research in Science Teaching, 15,* 465–478.

25. Neal, *Exhibits for the small museum,* 86.

26. Miller, G. A. (1956). The magical number seven, plus or minus two: Some limits on our capacity for processing information. *Psychological Review, 63,* 81–97.

27. Stapp, C. B. (1984). Defining museum literacy. *Roundtable Reports, 9*(1), 3–4.

Chapter 6

1. Graburn, "Museum and the visitor," 5–32.

2. Balling & Cornell, *Family visitors.*

3. Wagner, K. F. (1989). Maintaining a high quality visitor experience. In S. Bitgood, J. T. Roper, Jr., & A. Benefield (Eds.), *Visitor studies—Theory, research, and practice: Proceedings of the Second Annual Visitor Studies Conference* (Vol. 2). Jacksonville, AL: The Center for Social Design.

4. Ibid.

5. Ibid.

6. Falk, "Use of time," 10–13.

7. Consolazio, C. F., Johnson, R., & Pecora, L. (1963). *Physiological measurements of metabolic functions in man.* New York: McGraw-Hill.

8. Coles, R. (1975). The art museum and the pressures of

society. In *On understanding art museums* (pp. 189–190). Englewood Cliffs, NJ: Prentice-Hall.

9. Ibid., 197–198.

10. Falk & Balling, "Field trip milieu," 22–28.

11. Martin, Falk, & Balling, "Environmental effects," 301–309.

12. Wagner, "Maintaining a high-quality visitor experience."

13. Kimmel, P. S., & Maves, M. J. (1972). Public reaction to museum interiors. *Museum News, 51,* 17–19.

14. Wolf & Tymitz, *Whatever happened to the giant wombat.*

Falk, "Analysis of the behavior of family," 44–50.

Taylor, *Understanding processes of informal education.*

15. Hayward and Brydon-Miller, "Spatial and conceptual aspects of orientation," 317–332.

16. Stea, "Program notes on a spatial fugue."

Winkler, *Use of maps and guides.*

17. Stea, "Program notes on a spatial fugue."

Lynch, *Image of the city.*

18. Hayward & Brydon-Miller, "Spatial and conceptual aspects of orientation," 317–332.

19. Ibid., 317–332.

20. Wagner, "Maintaining a high quality visitor experience."

21. Monmaney, T. (1987). Are we led by the nose? *Discover, 8*(9), 48–56.

22. Wagner, "Maintaining a high quality visitor experience."

23. Ibid.

24. Liles, K. H., & Roth, S. E. (1978). The unrelated business income problems of art museums. *Connecticut Law Review, 10*(3), 638–652.

25. Falk & Dierking, "Effect of visitation frequency," 94–103.

26. Graburn, "Museum and the visitor," 5–32.

27. Newman, *Insights: Museums.*

28. Yellis, *Reverence, association, and testing.*

29. Eyl, J. V. (1991). *"Court Arts of Indonesia" at the Arthur M. Sackler Gallery.* Unpublished manuscript.

30. Falk, "Museum recollections," 60–65.

Falk & Dierking, "Effect of visitation frequency," 94–103.

Chapter 7

1. Hicks, E. C., & Munley, M. E. (Eds.). (1985). *Museums for a new century.* Washington, DC: American Association of Museums.

American Association of Museums. (in press). *Excellence and equity: Education and the public dimension of museums, A report on the Task Force on Museum Education.* Washington, DC: Author.

2. Screven, *Measurement and facilitation of learning.*

Screven, C. G. (1975). The effectiveness of guidance devices on visitor learning. *Curator, 18*(3), 219–243.

Shettel, "Exhibits: Art form or educational," 32–41.

Shettel et al., "Strategies."

DeWaard, R. J., Jagmin, N., Maistro, S., & McNamara, P. (1974). Effects of using programmed cards on learning in a museum environment. *Journal of Educational Research, 67,* 10.

Lakota, *National Museum of Natural History.*

Nahemov, "Research in a novel environment," 81–102.

Weiss, R. S., & Bourtourline, S., Jr. (1963). The communication value of exhibits. *Museum News, 42*(3), 23–27.

Brown, W. S. (1979). The design of the informal learning environment. *Gazette, 12*(4), 4–10.

3. Koran, J., Jr., & Baker, S. D. (1979). Evaluating the effectiveness of field experiences. In M. B. Rowe (Ed.), *What research says to the science teacher* (Vol. 2, pp. 50–64). Washington, DC: National Science Teachers Association.

Bitgood, S. (1989). School field trips: An overview. *Visitor Behavior, 4*(2), 3–6.

4. Boggs, D. L. (1977). Visitor learning at the Ohio Historical Center. *Curator, 20*(3), 205–214.

Borun, *Measuring the immeasurable.*

Balling, Falk, & Aronson, "Pre-trip orientations."

Birney, *Comparative study of children's perceptions.*

Delaney, A. A. (1967). An experimental investigation of the effectiveness of the teacher's introduction on implementing a science field trip. *Science Education, 5*(5).

Mahaffey, B. D. (1969). *Relative effectiveness and visitor preference of three audio media for interpretation of an historic area* (Tech. Rep. No. 1). Texas Agricultural Experiment Station.

Falk, *Understanding audience behavior and learning.*

5. Bransford, *Human cognition.*

6. Hein, G. (1991, May). *Does learning describe what happens to the casual visitor?* Paper presented at the 86th Annual Meeting of the American Association of Museums, Denver, CO.

7. Gardner, H. (1983). *Frames of mind: The theory of multiple intelligences.* New York: Basic Books.

8.———. (1985). *The mind's new science: The history of cognitive psychology.* New York: Basic Books.

9.———. (1991). *The unschooled mind. How children think and how schools should teach.* New York: Basic Books.

10. McCarthy, B. (1980). *The 4MAT system: Teaching to learning styles with right/left mode techniques.* Chicago: Excel.

———. (1983). *4MAT system in action: Creative lesson plans for teaching to learning styles with right/left mode techniques.* Chicago: Excel.

———. (1987). *4MAT workbook: Guided practice in 4MAT lesson and unit planning.* Chicago: Excel.

Gilbert, E. R. (1991). Using the learning style inventory. *Journal of Museum Education, 16*(1), 7–9.

11. Kolb, D. A. (1984). *Experiential learning: Experience as the source of learning and development.* Englewood Cliffs, NJ: Prentice-Hall.

Kolb, D. A., & Smith, D. M. (1986). *User's guide for the Learning Style Inventory: A manual for teachers and trainers* (pp. 35–37). Boston: McBer.

12. McCarthy, *4MAT system.*

McCarthy, *4MAT in action.*

McCarthy, *4MAT workbook.*

13. Bloom, B. S. (Ed.). (1956). *Taxonomy of educational objectives: The classification of educational goals. Handbook I: The cognitive domain.* New York: David Mckay.

Krathwohl, P. R., Bloom, B. S., & Masia, B. B. (1964). *Taxonomy of educational objectives. Handbook II: Affective domain.* New York: David McKay.

Bloom, B. S., Hastings, J. T., & Madaus, G. F. (Eds.). (1971). *Handbook of formative and summative evaluation of student learning.* New York: McGraw-Hill.

14. Czikszentmihalyi, M., & Rochberg-Halton, E. (1981). *The meaning of things: Domestic symbols and the self.* New York: Cambridge University Press.

15. Bower, G. H. (1981). Mood and memory. *American Psychologist, 36*(2), 129–148.

16. Maslow, A. H. (1954). *Motivation and personality.* New York: Harper & Row.

Rogers, C. R. (1951). *Client-centered therapy.* Boston: Houghton-Mifflin.

17. Maslow, *Motivation and personality.*

18. Rogers, *Client-centered therapy.*

19. Maehr, M. (1989, April). *The role of motivation in learning.* Paper presented at the annual meeting of the National Association for Research in Science Teaching, San Francisco, CA.

20. Beardsley, M. C. (1982). In M. J. Wreen & D. M. Callen (Eds.), *The aesthetic point of view.* Ithaca, NY: Cornell University Press.

21. Czikszentmihalyi & Rochberg-Halton, *The meaning of things.*

22. Ibid.

23. Chambers, M. (1990). Beyond "aha!": Motivating visitors. In B. Serrell (Ed.), *What research says about science learning in informal settings.* Washington, DC: Association of Science and Technology Centers.

24. Bruner, J. (1962). *On Knowing: Essays for the left hand.* Cambridge, MA: Belknap.

25. Graetz, L. (1984). Meaning-making and art. *Houston Art Scene, 5*(2), 3.

26. Brown, J. S. (1989, October). *Situated learning.* Paper presented at the Smithsonian Resident Associates Program, Washington, D.C.

27. Lewin, K. (1962). *Field theory in social science: Selected theoretical papers.* London: Harper & Row.

28. deGroot, A. D. (1965). *Thought and choice in chess.* The Hague: Mouton.

Chase, W. G., & Simon, H. A. (1973). The mind's eye in chess. In W. G. Chase (Ed.), *Visual information processing.* New York: Academic Press.

29. Chase & Simon, "The mind's eye."

30. McDermott, M. (1988). Through their eyes: What novices value in art experiences. In *Annual Meeting Sourcebook.* Washington, DC: American Association of Museums.

31. Borun, M. (1991, April). *Confronting naive notions through interactive exhibits.* Paper presented at Museum Education Roundtable Research Colloquium, Washington, DC.

32. Chase & Simon, "The mind's eye."

33. Falk, "Use of time," 10–13.

34. Bower, G. H., Mood and memory. *American Psychologist, 36*(2), 129–148.

35. Cohen, D. H. (1986). *Memory systems of the brain* (p. 27). New York: Guilford.

36. Bransford, *Human cognition.*

Harth, E. (1982). *Windows on the mind.* New York: William Morrow.

Thompson, R. F. (1986). The neurobiology of learning and memory. *Science, 233,* 941–947.

Norman, D. (1988). *The psychology of everyday things.* New York: Basic Books.

37. Squire, L. R. (1986). Mechanisms of memory. *Science, 232,* 1612–1620.

38. Ibid.

39. Restak, R. M. (1984). *The brain.* Toronto: Bantam Books.

40. Bower, "Mood and memory," 129–148.

41. Bransford, *Human cognition.*

Harth, *Windows on the mind.*

42. Bransford, *Human cognition.*

43. Ibid.

44. Vygotsky, L. S. (1978). *Mind in society: The development of higher psychological processes.* Cambridge, MA: Harvard University Press.

Bandura & Walters, *Social learning.*

Bonner, J. T. (1980). *The evolution of culture in animals.* Princeton, NJ: Princeton University Press.

Hinde, R. A. (1974). *Biological basis of human social behavior.* New York: McGraw-Hill.

45. Chase, R. A. (1975, September/October). Museums as learning environments. *Museum News,* pp. 36–43.

46. Lave, J. (1977). Cognition consequences of traditional apprenticeship training in West Africa. *Anthropology and Education Quarterly, 8,* 177–180.

Lancy, D. (1980). Becoming a blacksmith in Gbarngasuakwelle. *Anthropology and Education Quarterly, 8.*

Kimball, S. T. (1974). *Culture and the educative process: An anthropological perspective.* New York: Teachers College Press.

Damon, W. (1981). Exploring children's social cognition on two fronts. In J. H. Flavell & L. Ross (Eds.), *Social cognitive development: Frontiers and possible futures.* Cambridge: Cambridge University Press.

Greenfield, P. M. (1984). A theory of the teacher in the learning activities of everyday life. In B. Rogoff & J. Lave (Eds.), *Everyday cognition* (pp. 117–138). Cambridge, MA: Harvard University Press.

47. Vygotsky, *Mind in society.*

48. Koran, "Use of modeling," 285–291.

49. Bandura & Walters, *Social learning.*

50. Ibid.

51. Diamond, *Social behavior.*

Dierking, *Parent-child interactions.*

Birney, *Comparative study of children's perceptions.*

McManus, "It's the company you keep."

Hilke & Balling, *Family as a learning system.*

52. Dierking, "Family museum experience," 9–11.

53. Dierking, *Parent-child interactions.*

54. Gennaro, E., & Heller, P. (1983). Parent and child learning: A model for programs at informal science centers. *Roundtable Reports, 8,* 4–5.

55. Kelly, J. R. (1977). Leisure socialization: Replication and extension. *Journal of Leisure Research, 9,* 121–132.

56. Bell, P. A., Fisher, J. D., & Loomis, R. D. (1978). *Environmental psychology.* Philadelphia: W. B. Saunders.

David, T. G., & Wright B. D. (Eds.). (1975). *Learning environments.* Chicago: University of Chicago Press.

57. Jenkins, J. J. (1974). Remember that old theory of memory? Well, forget it! *American Psychologist, 29,* 785–795.

58. Rumelhart, D. E., McClelland, J. L., & the PDP Research Group. (1986). *Parallel distributed processing: Exploration in the microstructure of cognition. Volume 1: Foundations.* Cambridge, MA: MIT Press.

McClelland, J. L., Rumelhart, D. E., & the PDP Research Group. (1986). *Parallel distributed processing: Exploration in the microstructure of cognition. Volume 2: Psychological and biological models.* Cambridge, MA: MIT Press.

59. Bransford, *Human cognition.*

60. Falk & Balling, "Field trip milieu," 22–28.

Falk, Martin, & Balling, Novel field trip phenomenon," 468–472.

Martin, Falk, & Balling, "Environmental effects," 301–309.

Balling, Falk, & Aronson, "Pre-trip orientations."

61. Falk & Balling, "Role of context in learning."

62. Barker, *Ecological psychology.*

Barker & Wright, *Midwest.*

63. Norman, *Psychology of everyday things.*

64. Hiss, T. (1990). *The experience of place.* New York: Alfred Knopf.

Kaplan, S., & Kaplan, R. (1982). *Cognition and environment: Functioning in an uncertain world.* New York: Praeger.

65. Ausubel, D. P., Novak, J., & Hanesian, H. (1978). *Educational psychology: A cognitive view.* New York: Holt, Rinehart & Winston.

Chapter 8

1. Neisser, U. (1984). Memory revisited. In J. E. Harris & P. E. Morris (Eds.), *Everyday memory actions and absent-mindedness.* London: Academic Press.

2. Falk, "Museum recollections," 60–65.

Falk & Dierking, "Effect of visitation frequency," 94–103.

Fivush, R., Hudson, J., & Nelson, K. (1984). Children's long-term memory for a novel event: An exploratory study. *Merrill-Palmer Quarterly, 30,*(3), 303–317.

Wolins, I. S. (1991, May). *Children's memories for museum field trips: A qualitative study.* Paper presented at the 86th Annual Meeting of the American Association of Museums, Denver, CO.

Anderson, P., DeSena, A., Perry, D., Fialkowski, C., Siska, J., Edington, G., et al. (1991, October). *Preliminary research report: Museum impact evaluation study.* Paper presented at the annual conference of the Association of Science-Technology Centers, Pittsburgh, PA.

3. Falk, J. H. (1987). [Long-term museum recollections]. Unpublished raw data.

4. Fivush, Hudson, & Nelson, "Children's long-term memory," 303–317.

5. Wolins, *Children's memories.*

6. Falk, J. H., & Dierking, L. D. (1992). *Memories of early school field trips.* Unpublished manuscript.

7. Anderson et al., *Preliminary research report.*

8. Falk, "Museum recollections," 60–65.

Falk & Dierking, "Effect of visitation frequency," 94–103.

Falk & Dierking, *Memories of early school field trips.*

9. Fivush, Hudson, & Nelson, "Children's long-term memory," 303–317.

Wolins, *Children's memories.*

10. Gelman, R., Massely, C. M., & McManus, M. (1991). Characterizing supporting environments for cognitive development: Lessons from children in a museum. In L. B. Resnick, J. M. Levine, & S. D. Teasley (Eds.), *Perspectives on socially shared cognition.* Washington, DC: American Psychological Association.

11. Novak, J. D. (1985). Metalearning and metaknowledge strategies to help students learn how to learn. In L. West & L. Pines (Eds.), *Cognitive structure and conceptual change.* San Diego: Academic Press.

12. Neisser, U. (1982). *Memory observed, remembering in natural context.* San Francisco: W. H. Freeman.

13. Tulving, E. (1972). Episodic and semantic memory. In E. Tulving & W. Donaldson (Eds.), *Organization and memory.* New York: Academic Press.

14. Roediger, H. L., III, & Crowder, R. G. (1976). A serial position effect in recall of United States presidents. *Bulletin of the Psychonomic Society, 8,* 275–278.

15. Herman, J. F., & Roth, S. F. (1984). Children's incidental memory for spatial locations in a large-scale environment: Taking a tour down memory lane. *Merrill-Palmer Quarterly, 30*(1), 87–102.

16. Ibid.

17. Falk & Dierking, *Memories of early school field trips.*

18. Falk & Dierking, "Effect of visitation frequency," 94–103.

19. Ibid.

20. Falk & Dierking, *Memories of early school field trips.*

21. Falk & Dierking, "Effect of visitation frequency," 94–103.

Falk & Dierking, *Memories of early school field trips.*

22. Ibid.

23. Richardson, K., & Bitgood, S. (1986). *Validation of visitors' self-reports in a zoo* (Tech. Rep. No. 86–30). Jacksonville, AL: The Center for Social Design.

24. Norman, *Psychology of everyday things.*

25. Neisser, *Memory observed.*

26. Fivush, Hudson, & Nelson, "Children's long-term memory," 303–317.

Wolins, *Children's memories.*

27. Ausubel, Novak, & Haesian, *Educational psychology.*

28. Brown, R., & Kulick, J. (1977). Flashbulb memories. *Cognition, 5,* 73–99.

Bahrick, H. P., Bahrick, P. O., & Wittlinger, R. P. (1975). Fifty years of memory for names and faces: A cross-sectional approach. *Journal of Experimental Psychology: General,* 54–75.

29. Falk & Dierking, *Memories of early school field trips.*

30. Loftus, E. F., & Palmer, J. C. (1974). Reconstruction of automobile destruction. *Journal of Verbal Learning and Verbal Behavior, 13,* 585–589.

Chapter 10

1. Falk, J. H. (1991). *Front-end evaluation of the "Living Ecosystems" exhibition, National Museum of Natural History* (Interim Report). Washington, DC: Smithsonian Institution, National Museum of Natural History.

2. Ibid.

3. Newman, *Insights: Museums.*

4. Taylor, *Successful family experience.*

5. Thompson, C. (1991). Entertainment and education: Antonyms or allies? *Journal of Museum Education, 16*(2), 13.

6. Graburn, "Museum and the visitor," 5–32.

7. Weil, S. (1991, July/August). [Review]. *Museum News,* p. 63.

8. Anderson, L. L. (1991). Zoo interpretation and exhibit design: Two sides of the same coin. *Journal of Museum Education, 16*(2), 4–6.

9. Ibid, 4–6.

10. Conway, W. G. (1968). How to exhibit a bullfrog: A bedtime story for zoo men. *Curator, 11,* 310–318.

11. Finlay, T. W. (1986). *The influence of zoo environments on the perceptions of animals.* Unpublished master's thesis, Georgia Institute of Technology, Atlanta.

12. Greene, M. (1987, December). No RMS, Jungle Vu. *The Atlantic Monthly,* pp. 62–78.

Bitgood, S., Coe, J., & Yellis, K. (1991, May). *Exploring the visitor's immersion experiences.* Paper presented at the 86th Annual Meeting of the American Association of Museums, Denver, CO.

Chapter 11

1. Balling, Falk, & Aronson, "Pre-trip orientations."

2. Ibid.

3. Falk & Balling, "Field trip milieu," 22–28.

4. Wolins, *Children's memories.*

5. Gardner, *Frames of mind.*

6. McCarthy, *4MAT system.*

———., *4MAT in action.*

———., *4MAT workbook.*

7. Harvey, H. W. (1951). An experimental study of the effect of field trips upon the development of scientific attitudes in a ninth grade general science class. *Science Education, 35*(5), 242–248.

Gottfried, J. (1980). Do children learn on school field trips? *Curator, 23*(3), 165–174.

8. Shettel, "Exhibits: Art form or educational," 32–41.

9. Wolins, *Children's memories.*

10. Falk, J. H., & Dierking, L. D. (1992). *First experiences: Recollections of museum professionals.* Manuscript submitted for publication.

11. Martin, Falk, & Balling, 301–309.

12. Damon, W. (1984). Peer education: The untapped potential. *Journal of Applied Developmental Psychology, 5,* 331–343.

Slavin, R. (1983). *Cooperative learning.* New York: Longman.

Johnson, D. W., Johnson, R. T., Johnson E. H., & Roy, R. (1984). *Circles of learning: Cooperation in the classroom.* Alexandria, VA: Association for Supervision and Curriculum Development.

13. Wolins, *Children's memories.*

14. Falk & Dierking, *First experiences.*

15. Birney, *Comparative study of children's perceptions.*

16. Bitgood, "School field trips," 3–6.

17. Ibid.

Annotated Bibliography

Abadzi, H. (1990). *Cognitive psychology in the seminar room*. Washington, DC: The World Bank.

A very comprehensive overview of cognitive psychology designed for non-psychologists, with excellent sections on memory, thought, and problem solving. The use of comprehensible charts and graphs to explain complex phenomena is a noteworthy feature of this monograph.

Adams, G. D. (1989). *The process and effects of word-of-mouth communication at a history museum*. Unpublished master's thesis, Boston University.

Adams' market perspective on the museum experience demonstrates the importance of word-of-mouth in influencing visitor perceptions of museums. His literature review, highlighting years of research on product use and public perception, is particularly useful and complete.

Alt, M. B., & Griggs, S. A. (1984). Psychology and the museum visitor. In J. M. A. Thompson (Ed.), *Manual of curatorship: A guide to museum practice* (pp. 386–393). London: Butterworths.

This excellent article suggests that the behavioristic "model of man" used as a basis for the design of most exhibits is extremely inadequate and inappropriate when applied to museum visitors and has placed a misguided focus on the exhibit, and not on the psychology of the visitor. To truly understand the museum experience requires an understanding of people, not exhibits.

Anderson, L. L. (1991). Zoo interpretation and exhibit design: Two sides of the same coin. *Journal of Museum Education, 16* (2), 4–6.

A thoughtful and well-written article about interpretation that analyzes the various components of a successful experience for the zoo visitor. Anderson argues that interpreters and other zoo professionals need to consider more than just the information presented. How visitors perceive the design of enclosures and the neatness of the facility also strongly influence visitor experiences.

Bandura, A., & Walters, R. (1963). *Social learning and personality development*. New York: Holt, Rinehart and Winston.

This book describes a series of classic studies designed to demonstrate the importance of socially mediated types of learning. In particular, these authors demonstrate the importance of modeling and other non-verbal forms of learning within families and social groups.

Barker, R. G. (1968). *Ecological psychology*. Palo Alto, CA: Stanford University Press.

Barker, R. G., & Wright, H. F. (1955). *Midwest and its children*. New York: Harper & Row.

These two books are major works that resulted in the development of a whole new field of psychology—"ecological" psychology. The notion of behavior settings and the studies from which they were generated are described extensively.

Birney, B. (1986). *A comparative study of children's perceptions and knowledge of wildlife and conservation as they relate to field trip experiences at the Los Angeles County Museum of Natural History and the Los Angeles Zoo*. Unpublished doctoral dissertation, University of California at Los Angeles.

An important first attempt to study how sixth-grade children perceive museums and the social environment of these institutions and how these perceptions influence the acquisition of scientific concepts.

Bitgood, S., Patterson, D., & Benefield, A. (1986). *Understanding your visitors: Ten factors that influence visitor behavior* (Technical Report 86–60). Jacksonville, AL: Psychology Institute.

This report reviews a number of visitor behavior studies and provides a concise description of ten factors to consider in exhibit design that may result in more effective exhibits.

Borun, M. (1977). *Measuring the immeasurable: A pilot study of museum effectiveness*. Washington, DC: Association of Science-Technology Centers.

This work is an important milestone in thinking about the visitor experience and how to assess it. Borun provides examples of several different approaches to evaluating museum learning and behavior.

Bransford, J. D. (1979). *Human cognition: Learning, understanding and remembering*. Belmont, CA: Wadsworth.

In our opinion, this is one of the best books on learning ever written. Bransford provides both a historical perspective on learning research and a vision of the future in a thoughtful and easy-to-read style.

Brown, W. S. (1979). The design of the informal learning environment. *Gazette, 12*(4), 4–10.

Brown provides one of the first published attempts to distinguish clearly between informal and formal learning settings. This article presents a case study of an action research study in which one aspect of an exhibit is improved by using summative and formative evaluation techniques.

Cheek, N. H., Field, D. R., & Burdge, R. (1976). *Leisure and recreation places.* Ann Arbor, MI: Ann Arbor Science Publications.

These researchers were among the first to argue for an appreciation that museum attendance is a leisure-time activity freely chosen by the visitor. Their perspectives laid the groundwork for later work by Marilyn Hood and others.

Coles, R. (1975). The art museum and the pressures of society. In *On understanding art museums.* Englewood Cliffs, NJ: Prentice-Hall, Inc.

In this classic chapter, Coles argues that museums have not been open institutions, inviting people of all races and classes to participate. He points out some of the subtle, and not so subtle, messages that museum buildings, staff, and collections may communicate to minority groups within our society.

Conway, W. G. (1968). How to exhibit a bullfrog: A bedtime story for zoo men. *Curator, 11,* 310–318.

In this tongue-in-cheek article, Conway provides a vision for multi-sensory zoo exhibits that could appeal to a wide range of visitor interests and learning styles. Although somewhat dated in language, the points made and concrete examples provided remain timely.

Diamond, J. (1979). *The social behavior of adult-child groups in the science museum.* Unpublished doctoral dissertation, University of California, Berkeley.

An important first effort to use ethological techniques to study the family museum experience. The teaching behaviors of the family unit are particularly highlighted.

Dierking, L. D. (1989). The family museum experience: Implications from research. *Journal of Museum Education, 14*(2), 9–11.

This concise article discusses the research on the family

museum experience and its implications for practice, arguing that families use museums as social, behavior, and learning settings.

Dierking, L. D. (1991). Learning theory and learning styles: An overview. *Journal of Museum Education, 16*(1), 4–6.

Dierking provides a succinct overview of traditional views of learning and describes ten generalizations representing key factors in the learning process.

Falk, J. H., & Balling, J. D. (1982). The field trip milieu: Learning and behavior as a function of contextual events. *Journal of Educational Research, 76*(1), 22–28.

This is the third in a series of articles documenting the important role that perceived novelty has on children's field trip behavior. In this paper, Falk and Balling develop a model which defines the relationship among task learning, behavior, and novelty.

Falk, J. H., Koran, J. J., Dierking, L. D., & Dreblow, L. (1985). Predicting visitor behavior. *Curator, 28,* 249–257.

Falk, J. H. (1991). Analysis of the behavior of family visitors in history museums: The National Museum of Natural History. *Curator, 34*(1), 44–50.

In the first study, Falk and colleagues describe an effort to systematically study visitor time allocation during a museum visit and conclude that it is possible to predict how visitors will allocate their time during a museum visit. The second study describes a replication of these results in another, very different museum and suggests that visits can be distinguished by four predictable phases.

Falk, J. H., Koran, J. J., & Dierking, L. D. (1986). The things of science. *Science Education, 70,* 503–508.

In this philosophical paper, the authors argue that the unique aspect of museums is *things* and suggest that, in Piagetian terms, museums may represent the best device our society has developed for the transmission of concrete reality to large numbers of people.

Gardner, H. (1983). *Frames of mind: The theory of multiple intelligences.* New York: Basic Books.

In this book, Gardner proposes that there are seven intelligences that individuals possess, which shape the way they experience, process, and retrieve information. This book, written by a respected cognitive psychologist, is one of the first that questions many of the assumptions made by traditional learning theorists.

Graburn, N. H. H. (1977, June). The museum and the visitor experience. In *The visitor and the museum* (pp. 5–32). Prepared for the 72nd Annual Conference of the American Association of Museums, Seattle, WA.

In an address to the AAM, Nelson Graburn, a University of California, Berkeley, anthropologist, provided one of the first frameworks for understanding visitor motivations for visiting museums. He proposed that visitors come seeking reverence, association, and education.

Harth, E. (1982). *Windows on the mind.* New York: William Morrow.

Although this work is somewhat dated, Harth provides a very readable description of the brain's neurological functioning and organization that remains valid. This would be useful background reading for a layperson's introduction to this increasingly complicated subject.

Hayward, D. G., & Jenson, A. D. (1981). Enhancing a sense of the past: Perceptions of visitors and interpreters. *The Interpreter, 12*(2), 4–11.

This article provides an excellent example of how to include the affective dimension within an evaluation of a museum. Both the questions raised and the methodologies used in analyzing the data are worthy of study.

Hein, G. (1991, May). *Does learning describe what happens to the casual visitor?* Paper presented at the 86th Annual Meeting of the American Association of Museums, Denver, CO.

Hein presents a very cogent argument for utilizing constructivist approaches to understanding learning in both museum and school settings.

Hilke, D. D., & Balling, J. D. (1985). *The family as a learning system: An observational study of family behavior in an information rich environment.* (Final Report Grant No.: SED-8112927). Washington, DC: National Science Foundation.

This is one of several important studies on family visitors. Hilke and Balling's unique contribution is in considering the differences in family learning and behavior that result from interacting with different types of exhibits—e.g., static versus participatory exhibits.

Hood, M. G. (1983). Staying away: Why people choose not to visit museums. *Museum News,* pp. 50–57.

Hood, M. G. (1981). *Leisure criteria of family participation and non-participation in museums.* Unpublished manuscript, Hood Associates, Columbus, OH.

As outlined in Chapter 1, Hood did ground-breaking research on why visitors attend museums and why they do not; emphasizing museum visits as one of many possible leisure-time activities. In these two papers, Hood focused on art museum visitors, but her psychographic descriptions of visitor types seem applicable to any museum setting.

Koran, J. J., Jr., & Koran, M. L. (1986). A proposed framework for exploring museum education research. *Journal of Museum Education: Roundtable Reports, 11*(1), 12–16.

This article proposes a framework for museum education research that takes into account exhibit variables, individual characteristics of visitors, and intended outcome variables.

Koran, J. J., Jr., Koran, M. L., Foster, J., & Dierking, L. D. (1988). Using modeling to direct attention. *Curator, 31*(1), 36–42.

This article summarizes two studies conducted at the Florida Museum of Natural History that took research on modeling by social psychologists and applied it to the museum setting.

Laetsch, W. M. (1979). Conservation and communication: A tale of two cultures. *Southeastern Museums Conference Journal*, 1–8.

In this short article, one of the more frequently cited "obscure" articles in the museum field, Laetsch describes the inherent tension between education-oriented and collections-oriented museum professionals. He suggests that museums can most effectively communicate with the public by identifying the agendas of their visitors and eliminating rather than reinforcing the play/learning dichotomy of formal education.

Lakota, R. A. (1975). *The National Museum of Natural History as a behavioral environment—Part I—Book I.* (Final Report). Washington, DC: Smithsonian Institution, Office of Museum Programs.

This is one of the most thorough museum visitor studies ever conducted. Lakota's research characterizes both family and all-adult visitor groups, using multiple regression analysis to define important variables for each of these groups.

Loomis, R. J. (1987). *Museum visitor evaluation: New tool for management.* Nashville, TN: American Association for State and Local History.

Loomis's excellent primer on museum evaluation, although currently out of print, is worth finding if you want nuts-and-bolts guidance for designing surveys, leading focus groups, and conducting both formative and summative exhibition and program evaluation.

Mager, R. (1962). *Preparing instructional objectives.* Palo Alto, CA: Fearon.

This short volume provides guidance in developing sound, observable, and functional learning objectives. In addition to theory, it provides practice pages and step-by-step instructions.

McManus, P. (1987, June). It's the company you keep . . . The social determination of learning-related behavior in a science museum. *International Journal of Museum Management and Curatorship.*

After careful observation and conversation analysis of groups visiting the Natural History Museum in London, McManus concludes that the predominant variable affecting visitor behavior is the social interaction of the group.

Melton, A. W. (1972). Visitor behavior in museums: Some early research in environmental design. *Human Factors, 14*(5), 393–403.

A student of Robinson, Melton is one of the pioneers in the study of museum visitor behavior. He helped to make such terms as "holding power," "attracting power," and "museum fatigue" common in the museum literature.

Miles, R. S., Alt, M. B., Gosling, D. C., Lewis, B. N., & Tout, A. F. (Eds.). (1982). *The design of educational exhibits.* London: George Allen & Unwin.

An important anthology of articles about creating and evaluating effective educational exhibits.

Munley, M. E. (1986). Asking the right questions: Evaluation and the museum mission. *Museum News, 64*(3), 18–23.

This article outlines approaches to museum evaluation that should result in a better match between visitor agendas and museum missions.

Neal, A. (1976). *Exhibits for the small museum: A handbook.* Nashville, TN: American Association for State and Local History.

Neal's book is still a timely primer on the nuts and bolts of designing museum exhibits. This book is recommended even to those who are not in the business of designing exhibits.

Neisser, U. (1967). *Cognitive psychology.* New York: Appleton-Century-Crofts.

Like Bransford's *Human Cognition,* this book provides a comprehensive overview of the field of cognitive psychology. Neisser's notions of perception and recollection are particularly important contributions to the field.

Norman, D. (1988). *The psychology of everyday things.* New York: Basic Books.

An off-beat, but thought-provoking, book on how people react to the everyday items in their environment, from door handles to VCRs. The book includes important insights into how to design things for people that are both aesthetically pleasing and usable.

Rosenfeld, S. (1980). *Informal learning in zoos: Naturalistic studies of family groups.* Unpublished doctoral dissertation, University of California, Berkeley.

This was one of a few dissertations published in the 1980s that helped to provide some understanding of how families utilize and behave in informal learning settings such as zoos and museums. It includes some very rich naturalistic observations that are quite insightful.

Screven, C. G. (1986). Exhibitions and information centers: Some principles and approaches. *Curator, 29*(2), 109–137.

This comprehensive article focuses on several planning concepts and procedures, as well as certain psychological and behaviorial considerations underlying them, that affect the behaviorial and educational effects of exhibits on unguided visitors. It includes excellent sections on visitor motivation, evaluation as a tool for design planning, and visitor orientation.

Scribner, S., & Cole, M. (1973). Cognitive consequences of formal and informal education. *Science, 182,* 553–559.

The thesis of this article, by two well-respected anthropologists, is that school represents a specialized set of educational experiences discontinuous from those of everyday life, and that it requires and promotes ways of learning and thinking which often run counter to those acquired through practical daily activities.

Serrell, B. (1983). *Making exhibit labels: A step-by-step guide.* Nashville, TN: American Association for State and Local History.

This nuts-and-bolts primer on making exhibit labels includes up-to-date information from research and evaluation studies and tips for creating effective labels.

Shettel, H. H. (1973). Exhibits: Art form or educational medium? *Museum News, 52*(9), 32–41.

In this article, Shettel describes three categories of exhibit types: (1) those containing objects of intrinsic interest to visitors; (2) those containing objects that have aesthetic appeal to visitors; and (3) those with an instructional or educational role to play. He also argues for the use of formative evaluation in exhibition development.

Taylor, S. (1986). *Understanding processes of informal education: A naturalistic study of visitors to a public aquarium.* Unpublished doctoral dissertation, University of California, Berkeley.

An excellent, very readable dissertation on families that delves further into the museum experience as a social one and includes an interesting investigation of the visitor's perspective on questions and label copy.

Wolf, R. L., & Tymitz, B. L. (1981). *"Hey Mom, that exhibit's alive": A study of visitor perceptions of the coral reef exhibit, National Museum of Natural History.* Washington, DC: Smithsonian Institution.

One of a series of studies conducted by Wolf and Tymitz in which they advocate the use of naturalistic, visitor-centered perspectives on evaluating exhibitions.

Wolins, I. S. (1991, May). *Children's memories for museum field trips: A qualitative study.* Paper presented at the 86th Annual Meeting of the American Association of Museums, Denver, CO.

This paper describes a study that investigated the effect of museum field trips on children and the relationship these experiences have with the school curriculum.

ABOUT THE AUTHORS

John H. Falk, known for his work on learning in museums and formerly Director of the Smithsonian Office of Educational Research, has also served on the educational staffs of the Berkeley Botanical Garden and the Lawrence Hall of Science, Berkeley, and directed education at the Smithsonian's Chesapeake Bay Center for Environmental Studies. He is President of SLi, a non-profit educational research and museum evaluation company in Annapolis, Maryland.

Lynn D. Dierking, known for her work on families and learning, is Assistant Professor of Education at the University of Maryland and an adjunct lecturer in the Museum Education Program at the George Washington University in Washington, D.C. She has served on the educational staff of the Museum of Science, Miami, and the Florida Museum of Natural History in Gainesville, and has directed the Science in American Life Curriculum Project at the National Museum of American History.